ELEMENTARY DISCIPLINE HANDBOOK:

Solutions for the K–8 Teacher

ELEMENTARY DISCIPLINE HANDBOOK:

Solutions for the K–8 Teacher

Richard E. Maurer, Ph.D.

The Center for Applied Research in Education, Inc.
West Nyack, New York

Library of Congress Cataloging in Publication Data

Maurer, Richard E.
  Elementary discipline handbook.

  Includes bibliographies and index.
  1. Classroom management.   2. School discipline.
3. School children—Discipline.   I. Title.
LB3013.M37   1985   371.1′024   85-13229

ISBN 0-87628-296-6

Printed in the United States of America

To my parents,
my daughters Jeannette and Regina,
and my lovely wife Elizabeth.

About the Author

Richard E. Maurer, Ph.D. (Fordham University) is the principal of Anne M. Dorner Middle School in Ossining, New York. During his more than thirteen years in education, he has been a classroom teacher, school psychologist, and administrator.

Dr. Maurer has served for three years as national director of Project Intercept, a teacher training program sponsored by the U.S. Department of Education. He has also written articles for several professional publications that deal with peer counseling and evaluation, teacher evaluation techniques, and behavior modification skills, and has conducted many workshops for other educators.

About This Handbook

TEACHER: Billy, why don't you do your work?

BILLY: I *am* doing it.

TEACHER: You're talking too much. Open your book and get to work!

BILLY: Okay, okay.

Five minutes later, you look over at Billy only to discover that he hasn't done any more work than when you spoke to him. You call his parents that night to inform them of Billy's lack of progress, and they assure you things will change. The next day Billy completes all his work, but this trend lasts only a few days. By the week's end, Billy has reverted to his old routine of doing nothing. What can you do? How do you get Billy on task and working to his best ability?

Elementary Discipline Handbook will help you with all the "Billys" in your class. It will give you specific techniques that you can use immediately to produce positive and lasting behavioral change.

Have you ever wondered why the mood of your class can change from month to month? Why one month the students conform as a group to your rules and work hard; then the next month are restless, test you, bother each other, and accomplish little academically? How and why does a class mood change? Chapter 1, "Classroom Management Strategies," will show you how your class proceeds through four distinct group development stages during the school year. You will learn how to predict the *forming, storming, norming,* and *performing* moods of your class before any changes occur, and will learn specific management strategies that will let you take charge of the situation. The chapter provides twenty-four clear, concise strategies you can use throughout the school year to effectively control your classroom's group dynamics. Over fifteen classroom activities are also described that can be used to help your students get back to the task of learning and behaving appropriately.

In Chapter 2, "Discipline Strategies," you will find six different methods to change student behavior. You will see how to choose the right strategy for your needs and find out, step by step, how to implement that strategy. In most cases, you will even be told what to say to the student to produce the best and quickest solutions to the problem at hand. Numerous examples and illustrations show you how to apply these techniques in your own unique classroom situation.

Chapter 3, "Confrontation Strategies," describes the difference between confrontation and disciplinary goals, and demonstrates how to use a variety of verbal, nonverbal, and group confrontation tactics. Specific examples, with actual student dialogue, are provided to illustrate the mechanics of how to use these strategies. In addition, this chapter will demonstrate how to deal with student threats, an increasingly common phenomenon in many classrooms today. For those teachers who teach potentially out-of-control students, this chapter describes seven techniques which can be used to prevent a student from losing control and four action techniques that can be used immediately to help a student who is physically out of control gain composure. If you ever have been in a situation where a student is about to throw a temper tantrum or has actually "lost control," this chapter is required reading.

What is a master teacher? What does a master teacher do that makes him or her such an expert? Answers to these questions can be found in Chapter 4, "Instructional Strategies." Research has identified the teaching strategies that clearly reduce behavioral problems and promote increased student learning. Fourteen of these strategies are described and illustrated in the chapter. After reading it, you will be able to incorporate these strategies into your present instructional plans. Because they are the "nuts and bolts" of good teaching, they can be used by every teacher, regardless of curriculum content. How to question, where to move in the classroom, when to use a large class format as opposed to a seat work format, and how to reduce transition time are examples of how this chapter will enrich your instructional plan.

In many schools, teachers have no chance to visit each others' classrooms for the purpose of observing discipline, management, or instructional strategies. You may have wondered what some teachers in your building do that makes them so popular with parents and students. Chapter 5, "Peer Consultation: A Strategy for Professional Growth," describes one procedure you can use to effectively observe, analyze, and discuss what he or she does that works so well in the classroom. Nine suggestions and two examples are offered to help you implement this valuable strategy on professional consultation—a practice similar to that used in most other professions such as law, medicine, or sports.

As an added resource to guide you in locating and describing effective teaching strategies, two classroom observation instruments are provided in the Appendices.

Richard E. Maurer

How to Use This Handbook

Using the following five-step procedure will ensure not only that the particular discipline technique will be successful most of the time, but also that you will be able to adapt it to your own personality and classroom.

Step 1: Read

Read the technique you want to implement and determine what its particular outcome could be in your classroom. Compare and contrast this outcome with possible other outcomes you desire. Once you have decided you want this particular outcome, read the technique again for the specific process or steps involved.

Step 2: Practice

Practice the technique either to yourself or in front of a colleague. You may even consider a rehearsal by imagining yourself implementing the different stages of the technique and trying to guess what the outcome will be with different students in the class.

Step 3: Implement

Try the technique with a particular student or the entire class. If you are attempting a particular confrontation or discipline technique, first try it out on a student who is not your worst discipline problem. This gives you the opportunity to refine your technique before trying it on the toughest case. Or, you may want to use only part of the technique with a particular student or class. This gives you the opportunity to phase in the technique in different steps. (Most of the procedures described in this handbook can be implemented in such stages.)

Step 4: Refine

Refine the technique after your first few attempts by deciding what works and what does not work. Decide if the technique accomplishes your desired outcome. If not, try a different technique and discuss its merits with a colleague.

Step 5: Implement Again

Try the technique again. There is no better insurance than to know that you can repeat your performance. You may be surprised at how the implementation process can vary slightly with different types of students but still produce your desired outcome.

Many good resources are available that can supplement the implementation of your discipline program. These include:

Goodlad, John I. *A Place Called School.* New York: McGraw-Hill, 1983.

Joyce, Bruce, and Marsha Weil. *Models of Teaching* (2nd ed.), Englewood Cliffs, New Jersey: Prentice-Hall, 1972.

Lightfoot, Sara Lawrence. *The Good High School.* New York: Basic Books, 1983.

Ravitch, Diane. *The Troubled Crusade: American Education 1945–1980.* New York: Basic Books, 1983.

Rubin, Louis J. (ed.). *Improving In-Service Education: Proposals and Procedures for Change.* Boston: Allyn & Bacon, 1971.

The main point to remember as you use discipline and instructional techniques is that all of them can work for you and can make your classroom a better work environment. You probably will not adopt all of the techniques described in this handbook, but you will use many of them and, after adjusting them to your particular needs, find that they enhance your teaching performance and inspire your students' behavior and achievement.

Acknowledgments

The research and classroom observations which provided the basis for this book could not have been accomplished without the support and cooperation of a large number of people. In particular, I must acknowledge the aid of the teachers in the Ossining Public Schools (New York) who freely allowed me to observe, analyze, and provide feedback on their teaching performance. Their generosity was only surpassed by the excellence of their teaching. The administrators, directors, and principals of this district are to be commended for their critical and helpful evaluation of this research and observation methodology over the span of many years. In conjunction with Project Intercept, a National Diffusion Network teacher training program I direct, I had the opportunity to observe thousands of teachers from around the country. They provided many of the ideas, the opportunities to test and retest the techniques, and also the encouragement to write this book.

Contents

Classroom Management Strategies

CHAPTER 1

The first step toward achieving positive classroom discipline is the daily use of effective classroom management strategies. If you can appropriately manage a group of students during their academic tasks and through their social/emotional relationships, you can prevent many acting out behaviors, passive-aggressive acts, poor attitudes, lack of motivation, and general off-task behaviors from occurring.

Managing a classroom full of students, regardless of their age, takes courage, skill, and a knowledge of group process. Most teachers possess each of these three characteristics in varying degrees. While it is difficult to bestow the characteristic of courage, it is relatively easy to convey to teachers knowledge about group process and a description of skills that could be used to facilitate the classroom management process. This chapter will help teachers learn about group process as it relates to their classroom dynamics and gain a working knowledge of some teaching strategies which may be used to help manage this process.

FOUR STAGES OF A SCHOOL YEAR

Any time you put individuals in the same room and expect them to function together as a group, you have set the stage for a set of

1

behavioral dynamics which exceeds the personality characteristics of any single individual. This set of behavioral dynamics is often referred to as *group process*. In a classroom, group process may be seen as a series of developmental growth stages that a group of students moves along during the course of a school year. These stages are quite observable, can be predicted, and have implications for the teacher in terms of applying specific management procedures (Tuckman 1965). The four stages are briefly defined below.

FORMING	The stage in which students are introduced to and become familiar with the course content and with each other. Referred to by many as the "honeymoon."
STORMING	The stage of conflict and withdrawal in which students decide to distance themselves from the course and from each other. Referred to by many as "testing the limits."
NORMING	The stage in which students settle down and commit themselves to fulfilling the course requirements and to satisfying each other's social needs. Referred to by many as "settling in" or "gliding."
PERFORMING	The final stage in which students complete the course objectives, are provided with rewards and recognition, and begin to lessen their commitment to each other.

Every class of students shares to some extent the characteristics of each of these four developmental stages over the period of its existence. These stages are observable in classes at the elementary, secondary, and even college levels. Whether it be honors, special education, industrial arts, kindergarten through eighth grade, full semester, or half semester classes, virtually every type of class has some of the characteristics of these developmental stages.

No class goes through all these stages in the same pattern; however, although every group is different, each has identifiable stages. For example, a special education class for retarded children may not be able to move from the forming stage because its members are so dependent on the teacher for so many functions. A second example is in many gifted classes, where students move very quickly into the norming stage and then into the performing stage. Yet another example is an alternative school where classes can be stuck in the storming stage because students are unable to view others in the class as important. Many other variables influence the development stages of a class. A few are listed here.

- The class of students may be together some other time during the day and therefore be in another pattern of developmental stages progressing with another teacher.

- Vacation periods during the school year tend to make classes regress in their development. Information learned and social growth attained prior to a holiday period may need to be refreshed the first few days, week, or even month after returning.

- Some integrated curricula or team teaching schedules may make it necessary for you to start teaching a group of students who have been together for a period of weeks prior to your arrival. The class may have progressed through the initial stages of forming and storming without you. Your presence forces the group to readjust its pattern of behavior to include or, in some cases, to try to exclude you from feeling a part of their learning experiences.

- New students in your class usually are forced to start at the forming stage and make quick progress to catch up with the developmental pattern of the remainder of the class. Some students cannot catch up as quickly as other students or even you may wish. They present their own management needs.

- Many students can bring conflicting problems from home or the community into the class and as a result bring the whole class back to the storming stage.

- Your own personality and teaching style will affect how quickly a group progresses. For example, there are activities you can do which will facilitate the linking and information-sharing activities of the forming stage and therefore move the class along to some of the other stages.

This chapter describes a sequence of classroom development that is commonly reported by teachers. It is a consensus description, not a blueprint model, which you can use to precisely identify or control your own classroom group process. Since it is impossible to describe every developmental pattern that every class progresses through, it is hoped that you will use the description in this chapter to help you compare, identify, predict, and take control of the developmental pattern which is operational in your classroom at a particular point in the school year. Many of the charcteristics of each of the four stages will be valid for your students; some will not. You will have to make your own comparisons and contrasts. During the next school year, when you have a different group of students, you may want to reread this chapter to find if some of the characteristics of a particular stage have now become quite real for your new class. In any case, every one of the management strategies described here will help you manage each of the different stages your class will progress through.

HOW TO PREDICT THE MOOD OF YOUR CLASS

The four developmental growth stages of a class should be viewed from both a linear and cyclic perspective. On a linear mode, a class can move along a continuum during the course of a school year in a somewhat logical sequence. A typical school year may look like Figure 1–1. This development may not be typical of what you experience in your present situation. The forming period may extend further into October if you are in a large school in a large district. If your school enrollment is relatively low and the district small geographically, you may experience a shorter forming period. Many elementary and middle school teachers report that March can be a conflictive or storming time of the year. This is so because in many parts of the country at this time of year it is generally gray and overcast—even very cold and snowy—with no holidays to break the five-week month, and students can become restless. Therefore, a class which has moved into the norming stage may regress for a week or two and start showing characteristics of the storming stage during this period.

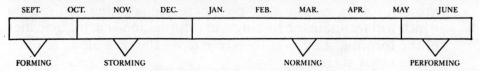

Figure 1–1. *Linear continuum.*

An alternative pattern of development reported by some elementary teachers is illustrated in Figure 1–2. The first month is a forming period followed by a short week of storming by testing the rules and regulations, followed by a long period of norming in which students settle down and work on task. A storming period may reappear again in February and March and the teacher may feel the need to tighten up on implementation of the rules and regulations. In April the norming period reappears again and students work right up to the final day of school. There is no formal performing period as such, but students do become involved during the school year in projects, plays, assemblies, or field trips which require that they apply their newly acquired knowledge in some form or other. These applications have all the characteristics of the performing stage with one exception—the time period is short. Students quickly "perform" their task and then move back to the norming stage. Bear in mind that generally a class moves along a linear sequence during the course of a school year, but may occasionally regress and demonstrate characteristics of an earlier developmental stage.

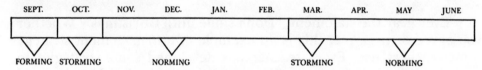

Figure 1–2. *Alternate linear continuum.*

A cyclic perspective can be gained by considering each developmental stage individually. Within each stage, students can behave by alternating between two separate functions—task functions and social/emotional functions (Bales 1950). Task functions are those which have to do with completing the job at hand such as studying, doing homework, and completing class assignments. Social/emotional functions are those which have to do with the relationships students have with each other and with the teacher. For example, in the norming stage of the school year most students will display task characteristics such as completing most class assignments, doing homework, or remaining seated at work for periods of time. Social/emotional characteristics would be demonstrated as students form new friendships or plan a party. During any one stage of development a class will shift back and forth between task functions and social/emotional functions. These shifts between task and social/emotional functions during a specific stage of class development can occur as often as every week or as infrequently as every month. The duration of time spent in each function may also vary. A typical comment from a teacher that her class was "a group of angels who completed all their assigned work last week, but a group of lazy socializers this week" can be explained by this cyclic view.

Always remember that there are two kinds of time being discussed when you consider classroom dynamics; the linear and progressive type and the cyclic and repetitive type. A classroom of students can be progressing during the school year from the forming stage through the performing stage, while at the same time alternating functions between task behavior and social/emotional behavior within each stage. This dual perspective will help explain why the behavior of students in a classroom is so difficult to understand and so time-consuming to manage. No wonder so many teachers have headaches at the end of the day!

MANAGEMENT STRATEGIES

Ever hear the statement, "Don't smile until Christmas"? Whether you agree or disagree, this is an example of a management strategy some teachers use. Every teacher has developed some strategies to manage their class dynamics. Through experience they have learned that at certain times during the school year certain activities are very useful for establishing control and for promoting achievement. A teacher who was recently recognized as the National Teacher of the Year claims he does no instructing for the first two days of school. He wants to get to know his students as persons first. Another teacher gives diagnostic tests twice a year to learn more about the academic performance of her students. Still others have parties, reward achievements, show entertaining movies, or go camping as part of their management strategy. After each of the developmental growth stages described here, you will find suggested management strategies which should help in moving your class through these particular stages. Use them to supplement your own strategies or even to become aware of strategies you use but do not know you use.

1. Forming Stage

The initial developmental stage is appropriately called the forming stage. During the month of September and into parts of October, the students are engaged in three primary activities: *linking, establishing rules and roles,* and *information seeking.* A teacher's comment seems to characterize aspects of this stage.

It took me the whole month of September to teach them what they should already know. By now they are finally ready for my course. It is amazing what they forget over the summer. September for me is review, review, review!

What this teacher is referring to is the process of linking students' knowledge, or more accurately, relinking students' knowledge, to the course material at hand. Linking activities are very evident in this stage because at the beginning of the school year everything about the class is being structured and established. The class as a whole is a collection of individuals searching for contacts with others who may know them or know their friends. Students look for others who may have been in their previous classes, those who live in the same neighborhood, those of the same ethnic background, or those with similar interests. Students interested in sports, in certain games, who dress alike, who live in the same apartment building, who like computers, science, and common hobbies will cluster. Some groups develop slang names such as "jocks," "preppies," "greasers," "whiz kids," and even stake out certain parts of the school grounds, cafeteria, or hallways as their "turf." Some teachers assign seats so there is little spontaneous interaction during the lesson (another example of a management strategy). Students still cluster, however, despite this structure because the dynamics of the group process are so strong.

As students search for common links, rules and roles are also being established. It is clear from the beginning that the only individual who has a set role and purpose at this stage is the teacher. It is the teacher who presents the rules, the course material, the textbooks, the general supplies, and even the time schedule. Generally, the class is in a very dependent state. The students need the teacher to form the structure of the class. Roles are initially established also. Those students who will become class leaders start to emerge as well as the class clowns, talkers, troublemakers, and solid workers.

The third activity is information seeking. Teachers seek information about the students in the form of giving diagnostic tests, reviewing school records, and talking to others who have had some of the students. Students seek information about each other and about the teacher. Personal issues about the teacher tend to fascinate students. Parents also seek information. Most back-to-school nights occur during this time period. Parents want to know what is being taught, why it is being taught, who is teaching it, and, most important, how their child compares to others in the class.

Characteristics of Task Behavior

- Students ask a lot of questions even when they know the answers. They are information seekers. The teacher is expected to provide answers, materials, and at times, the questions.

- Students attempt to discuss peripheral problems, search for the reasons they are in the class, and test the attending characteristics of the teacher for consistency.

- Most course requirements such as homework, staying in one's seat, and coming on time are completed. There is a honeymoon period in which the task at hand is completed.

- Students exchange information about themselves reluctantly. They avoid talking about past difficulties with you or giving opinions about course material. Much intellectualization takes place.

Characteristics of Social/Emotional Behavior

- Dependency on the teacher is significant. This, coupled with the tension and anxiety of individuals linking and seeking information, causes the class to scapegoat the physical environment, the school in general, or the principal as being in disfavor. The teacher is rarely challenged directly.

- Listening to others is not encouraged by students nor is it important to students. Interpersonal relations can be superficial. Students are primarily concerned about themselves in the class and their own personal relationship with the teacher.

- The class tests the teacher on which behaviors are acceptable. A student will come in late and everyone watches to determine how fair and consistent a teacher will be in rule enforcement.

- Most acting out behavior is exhibited as passive-aggressive in nature, rather than as outright hostility or aggressive acts.

Management Strategies

1. State your class rules in a clear and concise manner. For example:

No profanity

No food allowed

No wandering around

No music boxes, toys, or video games

Help "socialize" your class by explaining, demonstrating, and giving examples of the survival skills they will need to perform in your room. These skills will vary from teacher to teacher, but some common ones are how to line up; turn in homework; ask to leave the room; and behave during seat work, small group work, or large group activities. This socialization process usually takes from three to four weeks at the lower grade levels to one week at the higher middle school grade levels. It is best to avoid a discussion about rules and regulations for student agreement as this only raises the frustration and tension level of the new class. Students need to see you firmly in control at the beginning of the school year.

2. State the purpose and objectives of your course in a manner that relates to the needs and concerns of the individuals in your class. What is your course going to do for the individual student right in front of you? A course outline listing objectives and requirements should be handed out. A sample science course outline is shown in Figure 1–3.

3. Model the behavior you expect your students to display. Initially, they will be looking at *how* you do things more than at *what* you do. For example, if a student comes in late the class will be watching closely to see how you enforce the lateness rule. Will you scream, voice idle threats, bestow logical consequences, or ignore the infraction?

4. Establish a class meeting format where students can express their concerns about matters not related to instructional procedures. Instructional class time is not the time to handle complaints about the setting, rules, or relevance of your lesson. Some teachers hold class meetings each morning before the school day starts. Information is passed along, birthdays announced, and general housekeeping chores are handled before instruction starts. Other teachers prefer to hold class meetings at the end of the day, or only once a week, or even as infrequently as once a month. Some schools assemble the entire student body together in the cafeteria at the start of the day to make announcements, celebrate birthdays, and handle general complaints. Regardless of how, when, or where you hold the class meeting, it is important for students to feel there is a structured, planned outlet for their feelings.

5. A feedback board or large sheet of paper is helpful for students to express their feelings, both positive and negative, about material being studied. You can place large pieces of newsprint on the wall, ceiling to floor, and provide magic markers or crayons of all colors for

students to use. The advantage of this technique is that students can say things anonymously without fear of peer ridicule or teacher criticism. You should make a few rules, such as no profanity, no mocking of others, and no use of the board during instruction time. As the board gets filled with feedback you might take some class time to point out interesting comments and generate a discussion of their merits.

6. Activities of this stage, such as linking, establishing rules and roles, and information seeking can be facilitated and taken control of by the teacher if such exercises listed below are used on occasion. Each exercise, keyed to the particular stage, is described by stating the goal and explaining the procedures, often step by step, to follow. These exercises are designed to be completed in a 40- to 45-minute time period. Depending on the age and maturity of your students, you may want to alter aspects of a particular step so the procedures are valid for the students.

This year you will complete five units in science. Each Thursday you will complete a laboratory report. As a result of this course you will know more about the earth, the stars, your body, animals, and plants. A test will be given at the end of each unit.

1. *Introduction to the Scientific Method*
   A. Observation Methods
   B. Hypothesis Testing
   C. Experiments
      (Procedures, Safety, Equipment)
   D. Measurement
      (Metrics, Instruments)
   E. Reporting Data
      (Graphs, Reports)

2. *Earth Science*
   A. Weather and Climate
   B. Rocks
   C. Erosion
   D. Fossil Fuels
   E. Wind

3. *Chemistry*
   A. Atoms
   B. Equations
   C. Changes in Matter

4. *Biology*
   A. Microscope
   B. Cells
   C. Plants
   D. Worms
   E. Fish
   F. Humans

5. *Astronomy*
   A. Space Exploration
   B. Instruments
   C. Formation of Solar System
   D. Galaxies
   E. Stars, Planets, Moons, Meteors
   F. Fantasy and Fact

Figure 1–3. *Science: course outline.*

INTERPERSONAL DYADS (FS 1)

Goal

To introduce students to basic methods of developing interpersonal skills.

Procedure

Ask each student to pair up with another student. Have them select partners they don't know.

Once the dyads are formed, have one student from each pair interview the partner. Suggested questions might include, "What is your favorite group, record, course, color, hobby?"; "How many brothers and sisters do you have?"; "Do you have a boyfriend/girlfriend?"; and so on.

After two minutes have the partners switch roles (that is, the interviewer becomes the interviewee).

At the conclusion of the second interview (approximately two minutes), assemble the class into a large circle. Each student, one at a time, stands behind his/her partner and puts his/her hands on the partner's shoulders. The student then introduces the partner to the group by pretending to be that person. For example, "My name is Bob, my favorite group is the Grateful Dead...."

After everyone has introduced and has been introduced, encourage students to ask further questions of each other.

As a follow-up, ask your students how they felt during the introduction. It is important to examine student reactions and underlying feelings. (You should be aware that many students react negatively to this activity; they may become embarrassed or nervous during the introduction.) Meaningful discussions can result. Comments could be made about similarities and differences among students, and so forth. In addition, since listening is very important in this activity, you may ask students to comment on how hard or easy it was for them to listen and why.

CLASS PICNIC (FS 2)

Goal

To further develop feelings of trust and respect within the class unit.

Procedure

Planning and organizing the class picnic may take class sessions. Ask students to form a number of committees: setting up, fire-making, cooking, and cleaning up. Each student and teacher is asked to provide something to eat or drink. The food items should be assigned in a manner to avoid duplication.

Be prepared for the fact that students usually sign up for committees according to stereotyped roles. Try to avoid having all the boys sign up for setup and fire-making and all the girls for cooking and cleanup. It is preferable to have equal numbers of males and females on each committee. Another suggested rule is if a student forgets to bring a number of assigned items, he or she is barred from the trip.

Some time during the day organize a group activity (softball, volleyball, sack race). Group activities reinforce the concept of the class as a unit. Shared participation allows students to see each other and the teachers in roles outside the classroom. This broadened view, along with the results of team effort, further enhances student trust and involvement.

CLASS MURAL (FS 3)

Goal

To help students gain a better understanding of themselves and their abilities to interrelate with each other in the classroom.

Procedure

Plan and paint a wall mural. The project may involve a series of class sessions. Once the mural is started, however, students should be allowed to finish it after class or when they have completed the day's assignments.

Have each student stand in front of a light bulb (or slide projector) while another student traces the silhouetted shadow on the wall. The different silhouettes can be spread over the entire wall or placed high up the wall with the use of ladders.

After the silhouettes are completed, hold a class discussion on how to paint them. At this point, an art teacher should be called in for consultation or be assigned to help the class. This teacher could also help students in the painting process by offering ideas or touching up the finished mural.

Encourage the students to paint their silhouettes in a manner which best expresses them. For example, some students can paint pictures or symbols of hobbies, special interests, or horoscopes in their silhouettes.

The final mural should reflect student interaction. (Usually students connect themselves with one or another student in some fashion.)

The mural can remain all year and new students may be added when they enter the class. (It is advisable to use latex water-soluble paint.)

Alternative

Some classes may elect not to use a whole wall or to make the mural permanent. In such cases students could use ⅛-inch masonite board on which to paint themselves. These completed boards can then be hung from the classroom wall. Students may want to take them home at the end of the school year.

CLASS ATTITUDE EVALUATION (FS 4)

Goal

To help the students evaluate and express their attitudes about the class.

Procedure

Distribute the *Class Attitude Evaluation* form on page 16 and have each student rate the class on a four-point scale. Ask students not to identify themselves. Tabulate and post the results, using the summary results graph on page 17.

Elicit comments from the class about this evaluation. Discussing the evaluation results gives the students an opportunity to provide feedback on the course in a structured manner, while providing a situation in which they feel their opinions are important. Students learn that those with differing opinions are entitled to express themselves and that disagreement is accepted within the class.

This attitude evaluation can be given a number of times during the school year. Comparing the results will probably show changing student attitudes. Class discussions can be focused on these changes and what caused them.

CLASS ATTITUDE EVALUATION (FS 4)

Directions

Rate the class on each of the following items, using the four-point scale indicated.

1—Never/Not at All

2—Seldom

3—Sometimes

4—Often

————— 1. I am treated as a respected person in this class.

————— 2. I feel close to members of this class.

————— 3. There are cooperation and teamwork in this class.

————— 4. I trust others in this class.

————— 5. I feel my grades will be higher because of others in this class.

————— 6. I am honest in my relations to others in the class.

————— 7. The teachers here are fair in their dealings with me.

CLASS ATTITUDE EVALUATION (FS 4): SUMMARY RESULTS

Item	Average Score		Date			
1. I am treated as a respected person in this class.						
2. I feel close to members of this class.						
3. There are cooperation and teamwork in this class.						
4. I trust others in this class.						
5. I feel my grades will be higher because of others in this class.						
6. I am honest in my relations to others in the class.						
7. The teachers here are fair in their dealings with me.						

Directions: Rate the class on each of the following items, using the four-point scale:

1—Never/not at all
2—Seldom
3—Sometimes
4—Often

2. Storming Stage (SS)

The storming stage can begin at any time, but often takes place from the middle of October to about Christmas vacation. During this particular period there are a number of holidays such as Thanksgiving and Christmas, as well as special days of excitement, such as Halloween. Many teachers state that between Thanksgiving and the beginning of Christmas vacation there is an enormous amount of student acting out behavior evident as well as many students demonstrating feelings of depression. In some schools there are more student suspensions, referrals to the Committee on the Handicapped, and parent conferences. Guidance counselors, school psychologists, and school attendance officers find their referral list growing every day. One elementary teacher remarked

> It started gradually. First one would cry; then another would push going to lunch. I sent two students to the office today. I never send students to the office, but by the end of the day I realized they were becoming unglued. It seems every day now someone has a problem of some sort which occupies my time. I'm counseling more, teaching less.

This stage of class development is marked with *distancing* and *centering*. As the class members become accustomed to the class structure and procedure and to each other, they begin to feel the class starting to come together as a whole. Some students will resist this formation. They have yet to commit themselves to the course content or to the need to interrelate with others. These few begin to distance themselves by withdrawing from forming a commitment to the class. Homework is no longer done, tardiness increases, and the teacher is beginning to answer questions about why things have to be done in a certain way. The class is no longer dependent on the teacher. It is relatively easy for the teacher to characterize these students as being aloof, both from the curriculum and from others students.

As students distance, they start to withdraw into themselves. This activity is called centering and is the second process associated with the storming stage. During this stage of selfishness or preoccupation with "me," these students view everything that happens in the class, including social interactions, in terms of what it can do for them. If a teacher does something special for one student, they expect it to be done for all. If one of these students is singled out for not completing a class assignment, they are quick to recall incidents in which the teacher did nothing when others were caught. These students often argue with teachers about changing or bending the class rules for them and about altering the course content to meet their personal interests.

This centering activity is eventually bound to cause feelings of frustration and anger in these students because no teacher can be expected to fulfill all these individual demands. This frustration or anger that students feel displays itself in one of two ways. Either the frustration is turned inward and students become depressed, or it is turned outward and students become antagonistic. Depressed students are students who have turned their frustration inward. Teachers who deal with depressed students spend a lot of time listening, encouraging, giving advice, and persuading. Antagonistic students show their frustration in an outward manner. Passive-aggressive behavior or hostile acting out behavior is displayed. Teachers who deal with antagonistic students do a lot of confronting, disciplining, and removing students from classes.

During the storming stage, instructional time diminishes as the teacher must assume a managerial role to deal with various forms of distancing and centering activities. Students in the class who want to get on with the course curriculum are frustrated, angry, and bored with the amount of time not spent on instruction.

Characteristics of Task Behavior

- Complaints about the course content increase. Students show resistance or confusion about doing something a different way.

- Students begin to respect each other's opinions more, but generally only the opinions of those students they like.

- The pace of instruction slows down. Teachers do more managing and less instructing.

- Some students start to display negativity toward the course content. They reject parts of it, refuse to master other parts, and seek to alter course requirements.

Characteristics of Social/Emotional Behavior

- Interpersonal conflict is great. Students seek out those similar to them and ignore those who are different. Many dyad relationships are formed.

- Attempts to establish and maintain rapport with the teacher give way to building personal contacts in the class. The teacher is seen as less important than is, therefore, the classwork.
- Hostile students show anger by destroying objects, seeking fights, or vandalizing school property.

Management Strategies

1. Relate all personal attacks to the course content, to the school schedule, to the building, rather than to yourself. Try to remain objective to openly or passively aggressive actions. Students generally will accept your use of the confrontation and discipline strategies (discussed in later chapters) as a natural consequence of their acting out behavior. Rarely will they accept harsh anger or revenge from the teacher. Also, you may lose those marginally accepting students by such inappropriate reactions.

2. Be consistent and fair in your application of class rewards and punishments. Students are very aware of who gets rewards and who does not. Your credibility rests on your ability to be fair and equitable. Mention to the class that your goal is to remain fair, but that at times it is difficult to apply the same standard to every student all the time. Remind them that you are only human and although your judgments of reward and punishment may seem unfair to them at times, you are trying for consistency. Students will respect you for the attempt.

3. Remember to confront the behavior of the student, not the personality of the student. For example, say "Regina, you are a good student, but your lying about the homework upset me," rather than, "Regina, you really upset me."

4. Take students aside and explain your feelings about their individual behavior, what you would like changed, and why. Choose the worst behavior problem first and proceed through your list. Be sure to follow up your meeting with another meeting with the student a few days later to assess what, if any, change has been evident and to remind the student of your expectations.

5. Reduce class competition and encourage cooperation among students. The use of the "Jigsaw Classroom" technique (see Figure 1–4) is appropriate here because it forces students to rely on each other to complete the assignment.

6. Since students are distancing from each other and withdrawing more into themselves, it is appropriate to structure activities which

help students discover more about themselves. Once a stronger self-concept is developed, the students will more readily be able to move on to the next stage of development—the norming stage.

This example shows how the Jigsaw Classroom technique can be adapted for very young students. Rather than spend five full days on a task, and realizing that her students had more limited attention spans, Jan assigned only two class periods to this procedure. During the reading period on Monday, Jan formed six groups of four students. Each student in each group was given a copy of different paragraphs from a book. For every group of four students there were four paragraphs forming a complete story. Each student had to silently read his/her paragraph and then discuss the contents with the other group members. Each student was responsible for picking out the main idea and two key vocabulary words from his/her paragraph. This information was shared with other members of the group. During Tuesday's reading period, Jan asked the students to reform into groups and continue to discuss the readings of yesterday. Students were requested to review the four main ideas from each of the four paragraphs and to review the eight key vocabulary words from the four paragraphs. At the end of the reading period, the teacher handed out a quiz on the story. Each student was required to complete the quiz, which focused on identifying main ideas and defining key words in the story. Only those groups whose average score of four students was above 85 percent were awarded a prize. In this case, Jan was able to give cartoon character stickers to students in five of the six groups.

Figure 1–4. *A Jigsaw example.*

THE JIGSAW CLASSROOM*

Goal

This teaching strategy uses every student in the classroom as a resource for every other student. Interdependence is encouraged; competition, distancing, and centering are counterproductive to a student's achieving success, and therefore discouraged. To complete the task and get a good grade every student must listen to, respect the opinion of, and cooperate with every other student. Teachers who have used this technique have reported students' gaining more respect for others in the class, greater interracial cooperation, increased individual self-esteem, and, most important, greater mastery of classroom material. The strategy employs multimodal and multiformat instructional strategies which are described in Chapter 4 as effective for increasing student achievement.

Procedure

A class of thirty students should be divided into five groups of six students each. Each group will work separately as a team. On Monday you should instruct students on the new material or new concept. On Tuesday each team will meet in separate parts of the classroom. Inform each team that on Friday there will be a test on the new course material. Each person in a group will be given a separate assignment to research and is responsible for instructing other students in the group on his or her respective topic. The test will cover all the material so the research of each student on the team is important if everyone is to receive a good grade.

On Tuesday and Wednesday allow students to research their topics either in the school library or in the classroom. If the general topic is the major historical figures of the American Revolutionary War period, then within each team of six students there will be six separate historical persons to be researched. On Thursday allow each team to gather for individual students to instruct each other on the facts of the particular person each one researched. You will find that every student will listen attentively for the details. On Friday give the same test to every student. The questions should cover all of the material.

---

*Elliot Aronson et al, *The Jigsaw Classroom*, Sage Publications, Inc. 1978.

The reason this procedure is referred to as a "jigsaw" is because, as in a jigsaw puzzle, each student on the team has researched a part of a topic which, when combined with other parts researched by other students, completes a total picture.

SELF-COLLAGE (SS 1)

Goal

To help students develop a clear view of themselves and an ability to present this self-image to others.

Procedure

Allow two class periods. Ask each student to create a collage of pictures and/or words which is representative of him- or herself. The first class session may be used for actually making the collages (thumbing through magazines, cutting and pasting); the second for discussing them.

Students usually enjoy this activity, but they may require some help in deciding what pictures or words actually describe themselves. You may want to do some individual counseling during this activity to help students focus on themselves. Classmates may also be helpful in giving some insights.

Once all the collages are finished, ask each student to stand in front of the class and describe his/her collage. Questions like, "Why do you think a particular picture describes you?" are helpful to get the reluctant speaker going.

After all the presentations are completed, summarize the activity by pointing out similarities and differences in the collages. The collages may be displayed in the room for students to view and comment on at a later date.

TIME LINE (SS 2)

Goal

To show students that although their personal histories are different, they all share the same basic realities of life: (1) needs, (2) loves, (3) challenges, (4) beliefs, and (5) joys.

Procedure

Prepare a life chart. The chart should be large enough so that it is visible to all the students. On the chart list the most important events of your life and the year the event took place. For example:

1964—graduated from high school
1965—owned my first car
1967—involved in peace movement
1968—graduated from college
1968—first boyfriend/girlfriend that lasted a year
1969—first full-time job

Call attention to the time line and explain what it is. Give the participants a few minutes to read it over.

Ask if any see a particular date or person listed which has a special significance to them. Get a few answers and ask them why they are significant.

After several participants have answered, ask them all to write a personal time line on a piece of paper, starting with the date they first consciously remember as significant to them. They should list dates and events or people which influenced their lives in some way.

When sufficient time has elapsed ask them to break into small groups to discuss the time line. They should explain their charts to each other and tell each other which date they think is the most significant. Tell them to look for impact and perhaps something or someone which changed the direction of their lives.

After about ten minutes get the class back together and encourage them to share some of their findings with the whole group. Keep in mind that your aim is to demonstrate that our own personal and individual history can tell us something about who we are and our relationship with others. As the answers come out you will be able to categorize them on the blackboard under titles of needs, loves, challenges, beliefs, and joys.

Encourage the students to recognize the categories of their own examples. This activity should have demonstrated to the students that the same basic realities of their life are shared by others in the classroom.

HOW DO YOU FEEL TODAY? (SS 3)

Goal

To help students recognize certain feelings which affect their school-work and to help them change these feelings.

Procedure

Ask students to circle the number on each continuum that is closest to the way they feel right now.

When they finish, ask the students to share their results with the class. It may be interesting to note if any one particular feeling is prevalent.

Then ask each student to pick one or two feelings that he/she wishes to change and to circle that area.

Have the students form pairs and share those feelings with each other. Most students are reluctant to share the whole rating sheet, but usually one area can be revealed with little difficulty. Ask each partner to help brainstorm, listing things he/she could say or do today to change that feeling to the desired state. Encourage the process of brainstorming and, if possible, offer examples of how a feeling can be changed.

Form the pairs again the next day to check on the progress of the change.

HOW DO YOU FEEL TODAY? CONTINUUM (SS 3)

Directions

Circle the number on each continuum that is closest to the way you feel right now.

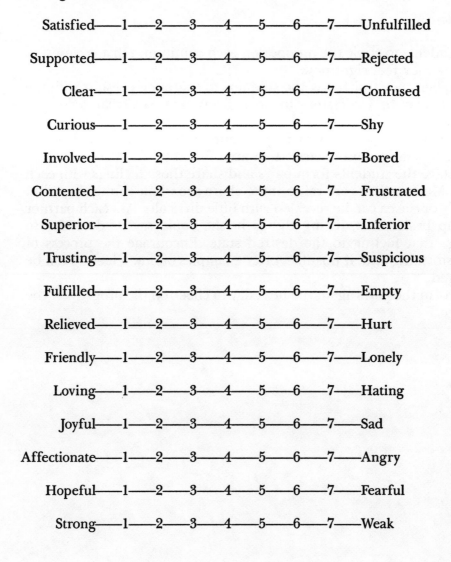

Satisfied——1——2——3——4——5——6——7——Unfulfilled

Supported——1——2——3——4——5——6——7——Rejected

Clear——1——2——3——4——5——6——7——Confused

Curious——1——2——3——4——5——6——7——Shy

Involved——1——2——3——4——5——6——7——Bored

Contented——1——2——3——4——5——6——7——Frustrated

Superior——1——2——3——4——5——6——7——Inferior

Trusting——1——2——3——4——5——6——7——Suspicious

Fulfilled——1——2——3——4——5——6——7——Empty

Relieved——1——2——3——4——5——6——7——Hurt

Friendly——1——2——3——4——5——6——7——Lonely

Loving——1——2——3——4——5——6——7——Hating

Joyful——1——2——3——4——5——6——7——Sad

Affectionate——1——2——3——4——5——6——7——Angry

Hopeful——1——2——3——4——5——6——7——Fearful

Strong——1——2——3——4——5——6——7——Weak

3. Norming Stage

This stage of class development is typically the longest and—unlike the storming stage in which social/emotional functions are dominant—the period in which most of the classwork and task functions occur. For a class that is a year long, the period often extends from January through May, with minor setbacks occurring around mid-winter and spring breaks. A remark from an elementary school teacher illustrates what can happen during this stage.

> I don't know what happened to these boys and girls. They are gems! Look at the work they have done. Not one student failed last week's spelling test. I wish I had this group last year. I wouldn't have had as many gray hairs. I have the A group helping students in the C group, something I would not have dreamed about last October.

This stage is marked with *orienting* and *fueling* activities. Students at this time start to orient themselves to the course curriculum and each other. With regard to the course, they begin to sequence the new course material, trying to recognize and label it in terms of past information acquired. They search for a logic or purpose to the new information and do this by developing internal cognitive images of the information. These cognitive images are critical orientation maps, since they help the student process and comprehend the new information much more readily and thoroughly. Previously acquired knowledge is pulled in, a future perspective is developed, and immediate goals are formed.

Bridie, for example, took biology as part of her fourth grade general science class. In seventh grade she took a full year of biology and became quite interested in the function of DNA. With the help of her teacher she was able to recall and relate general information learned in other classes to the specifics of understanding DNA.

All these experiences contributed pieces of information which she could draw together to help her begin to understand DNA. She had started to make the process her own by developing an internal cognitive image of what DNA was all about. As this stage of class development proceeds, Bridie will have the opportunity to have her image further developed and tested by the task and social/emotional experiences of the class.

Students also orient themselves to each other during this stage. Roles assumed and assigned earlier in the school year are now a permanent part of each individual student's expected behavior. Most actions of individuals are viewed within the role-image that person has established. For example, students who ask a lot of questions, argue, come late, procrastinate, clown around, lead discussions, show off, flirt, withdraw, and so on, are well known. Students have so well oriented themselves to each other that when a student demonstrates behavior not congruent with his or her role, he or she is perceived as "acting strange." Some students refer to such incongruent behavior as "acting gross," meaning the person is not him- or herself.

A second activity which occurs during this stage is that of fueling. Fueling is the process an individual uses to gather and store the necessary energy and materials to complete the course requirements and to participate in the classroom social activities. Regarding the task functions, students first assess their needs to determine what strengths they can draw upon to fulfill the requirements of the course. They might judge whether they have the intelligence to comprehend the course material and how they rank compared to others in the class. Some look at their weaknesses and wonder if these are formidable enough to prevent them from completing the requirements. They may even determine what grade they will achieve in the course if they commit such and such amount of time and energy to studying.

The second step is for students to survey where they may gather additional energy or help to complete the task. Some may ask older students what kind of grades the teacher gives and where they can get extra help. The third step is for students to request additional help. They ask for extra work, ask peers to assist them, see the guidance counselor, attend extra help sessions after school, or even arrange for a tutor to help them. Some decide to ask their parents for a computer, a typewriter, or even some private room in which to do homework.

Fueling can be seen on the social scene as well. Students assess, survey, and request additional help to interact with each other. Boys are attracted to particular girls and girls to particular boys. Going steady may even take place during this stage of social/emotional development among older children. A girl may decide if she has the personality, looks, and interests to attract a certain boy. She surveys where she can gain additional help such as changing her dress style, her seat, or her greeting. She then picks one or more of these changes to execute to see if she can attract the boy's interest.

Characteristics of Task Behavior
- There is a general openness to class discussions.

- Individuals talk about themselves and others. There is more listening to others' views and, as a result, more interpretations of the facts are available.
- Class activities are assigned based on the skill of members to determine each other's competencies and weaknesses.
- Students challenge those who do not do the work and who, therefore, keep the class behind. Rewards and punishments are developed to maintain the norms of the class.
- The teacher's personal opinion is often requested.

Characteristics of Social/Emotional Behavior

- There is a development of group cohesion. Dyads are less important as members seek new friends.
- Conflicts between class members are avoided as much as possible; harmony is important.
- Individual members assume certain roles. Some roles are sought after; others are given by the group.
- Personality traits of the students are identified and are predictable by both students and teachers.

Management Strategies

1. This is an opportunity for presenting the most conceptually difficult part of your course content. Students are prepared to do more homework and class assignments oriented toward understanding the content. On a weekly basis, remind students of and reinforce the purpose of your course, the objectives of lessons, and the requirements for successful completion of the course. This process is referred to as "teaching to form the image" and is discussed at length in Chapter 5 on "Instructional Strategies."

2. Help students brainstorm and locate those people, places, and things they need to help complete your course.

3. Help students get to know you and each other better. Allow the class to plan activities such as a picnic, a field trip, or a breakfast together.

4. Ask for some feedback from the students on your course content regarding quality and quantity. A questionnaire form is appropriate because its results can be summarized quickly and reported to the class. This feedback helps the class understand what

others are thinking and feeling and will help the class orient itself to successfully completing the course requirements.

5. Renegotiate any class rules with which students have expressed displeasure since the beginning of the school year. You need not change, rules which you feel are essential for classroom discipline and performance, but at least students will have the opportunity to understand why you have such rules. For those rules you are willing to change, remind students that there are "gives to get." If you are going to bend one of the class rules, students should give something in return. For example, if you are going to allow students to bring food into the classroom, you may want to require that they do additional questions for homework.

6. Structure activities that allow individual students and sub-groups to exchange information. The use of the Teams-Games-Tournaments curriculum (page 31) is appropriate here.

7. Since students are orienting and fueling themselves during this growth stage, the use of the exercises at the end of this section on norming will assist students to complete these activities especially with regard to social/emotional functions.

TEAMS-GAMES-TOURNAMENTS

TGT is a complex but very interesting fun-filled activity for teachers to use with children at this stage of the class group development. To fully understand the operation of this activity, you should read Robert Slavin's *Using Student Team Learning.** Below is a synopsis of the activity which will provide you with an orientation to TGT.

Goal

This teaching strategy organizes the class into teams which will compete with each other during a game. A series of games over a period of weeks constitutes a tournament. Teams score wins for each game and the team at the end of the series with the greatest number of wins is awarded recognition through newletters or by displaying the students' names on the class bulletin board. The goal of this strategy is that students will help, listen, and respect other students. Peer teaching and support are essential ingredients for not only team success, but for increasing student achievement and for improvingstudent relations. This strategy is an excellent method to use when the class as a whole is ready to invest time and energy in learning new course material.

Procedure

Each team has four or more students representing a cross section of the academic ability of the class—some bright students, some average, and some below average. The teacher will have to construct each team carefully so that each team has an equal chance of winning. Typically, one or two class periods are used for the teacher to introduce the new course material. Then each team meets to study the material and coach each other on how to organize the facts and how to compute practice problems. Usually one or two class periods are devoted to this phase. The class period the next day is devoted to the tournament.

Your lesson plan to introduce the new material should teach the objectives to be tested by the game. Students will need to feel the urgency of learning the material you are introducing.

Team practice sessions are important because it is here that students learn to help each other learn the course material. Work-

---

*Robert E. Slavin, *Using Student Team Learning*, Center for the Social Organization of Schools, The Johns Hopkins University Team Learning Project, Baltimore, MD, 1980.

sheets which contain questions and anwers are provided for each student. Have students divide into subgroups of two or three within each team to quiz, explain, give further examples, and encourage each other to master the new material. No one is finished practicing on a team until everyone learns the material. Switch partners around on a team until you feel the material is being mastered and you feel a sense of "teamwork" is being established. Your role at this time is to circulate around the room and help with problems with the content or with the practice procedures.

During the game, each team sends a representative to the various gaming tables where course-related questions are asked of all students. Students of comparable ability are seated at the same table. This way students from each team are competing with students with similar academic ability. The prepared questions are drawn from the material studied earlier in the week.

Once at the gaming table, a student will pick a number from a deck of numbered cards. Another student from another team at the table will read the question which corresponds to the number drawn. If the student answers the question correctly, a point is gained. If the answer is incorrect, no point is lost. The student to this student's right may have the chance to challenge the response. A second challenge may also be conducted by the next student. The second student challenger checks for answer authenticity. Challengers should be careful—they can lose points for incorrect responses. After all questions are answered each team member totals his or her points and returns to his or her team to report and cumulate scores. The team whose members gain the most points wins the game.

Students have been known to enjoy this activity so much that teams often give themselves names, chants, newsletters, and banners. The competition can be keen, so students work hard at helping each other understand the material, encourage each other to succeed, and become very supportive of each other's needs. Over the course of the school year, many tournaments can be held with different teams being formed for each tournament. Students have the opportunity to work with almost every other student in the room. Curriculum to be included in TGT may cover most subjects taught in elementary schools: health, science, social studies, and English, to name but a few.

CIRCLE COMPLIMENT (NS 1)

Goal

To give students direct feedback on how they are perceived by others in the class.

Procedure

Arrange the class into a large circle. Have one student stand in the middle of the circle or sit in the chair with his/her back to the group. Each student in the circle offers a compliment to the student in the center. The student in the center faces each speaker until he/she receives a compliment from everyone and completes the circle. The compliments usually are of a personal nature like, "He is gentle," or, "She is friendly." Occasionally, students offer compliments about appearance or academic or athletic ability.

Each student should be encouraged to start in the middle. Though very "risky" for some students, this activity provides a high element of reward. Once the class concludes this activity, generally there is a feeling of elation. They should discuss their feelings about the activities. The teacher should guide the discussion.

MODIFIED CIRCLE COMPLIMENT* (NS 2)

Goal

To encourage positive exchanges between teacher(s) and students.

Procedure

Arrange the class in a circle. Ask each student to list all the other class members and to write at least one compliment next to each name. Have students exchange papers and read the list of names and compliments aloud. Discuss student reaction to the exercise.

---

*The Modified Circle Compliment can precede or follow the Circle Compliment depending on the development and attitude of the class.

SHARE A CONCERN (NS 3)

Goal

To give students an opportunity to receive peer support.

Procedure

Give each student a small piece of paper and ask them to describe a problem they are having currently. These concerns can be described in the form of a question. Students should be told that these concerns will be kept confidential.

Collect all the problems and concerns and put them into a hat or a box. Pass the hat so that each student draws a concern out of the hat. If a student draws his or her own concern, another one should be drawn.

One at a time, each student reads aloud the concern he or she has drawn. The other students then offer advice or suggestions on how to resolve this problem. Each student gets a chance to read the concern drawn and every concern is discussed by the class. Stress the right of confidentiality.

Although some students will identify their problems when they are read, others should not be pressured by their classmates to do so.

By receiving advice from others, a student is able to become aware of options or possibilities for future behavior change.

GROUP DISCLOSURE (NS 4)

Goal

To allow the students an opportunity to see how others in the class view them.

Procedure

Distribute the *Group Analysis Sheet* (shown on page 36). Ask each student to complete the sheet. Remind them not to put their names on the sheet nor to include themsleves in the ratings.

Collect the completed sheets and post them in the room for students to read. Analyze the sheets by counting the number of times a particular student appears in a category. The student could be asked how these opinions correspond to his or her own opinion. The students should be asked how they felt doing this activity. Pose questions such as, "Was it difficult to judge your fellow classmates?"; "Were you reluctant to look at how others judged you?".

GROUP ANALYSIS SHEET
(Group Disclosure NS 4)

Instructions

Answer all questions with first names only of two of the class members. Do not include yourself.

1. Who works the hardest in the class?   _____ _____

2. Who can easily influence others in the class?   _____ _____

3. Whom do you know the least?   _____ _____

4. Who do you think can help you the most with personal problems?   _____ _____

5. Who do you think causes the most upset in the room?   _____ _____

6. Who do you think should talk more in the room?   _____ _____

7. Who is the friendliest?   _____ _____

8. Whom have you gotten to know the most this year?   _____ _____

4. Performing Stage

The final stage of class development is probably the most rewarding for both teacher and student. This is the time when students start to demonstrate a working competency in the knowledge they have acquired during the school year. In some classes, particularly in the upper grades, this performing period can run from about May to the end of the school year in June. In other classes this period appears at intervals during the year. Some teachers spend this period providing no new information, but rather review the material previously covered. Other teachers often can be seen directing and supervising rather than actually instructing students on how to apply the recently acquired knowledge. Exams, a trip, a demonstration, or an application of some knowledge are usually seen during this period and are supposed to reveal how much a student has learned or retained in a particular time period.

In terms of activities, the performing stage is one of contradiction. While it is the time students can develop the greatest competency in use of course information, it is also the time when a great amount of activity is devoted to terminating the school year or a class activity. These remarks by teachers illustrate these opposing activities.

> After our school assembly, forget about making them work in class. All they wanted to do was to relax and talk about everything that had happened. They were so excited they could not work. It took two days before I felt we had a "normal" day.

> After the eighth grade dance they felt the school year was over. These students decided it was time to socialize and take final exams. They all knew they were going to high school in the district so there was little I could do to motivate them. They wanted to know only that which helped them on the exam. Some even planned to skip the last few days of school.

The two activities, therefore, that are associated with this period of class development are *mobilizing* and *disengaging* processes. All the energy and material resources stored or fueled during the norming stage are now mobilized for action. Students expend their energies and resources to complete course requirements.

First they budget their time and resources; then they distribute them among the tasks and social/emotional functions of the class. For example, if a term paper is required, students need to decide how, when, and where they will start to research, write, and type this paper.

They budget and distribute their resources as to have the paper completed by the due date. On other assignments and final exams they decide how much they must contribute or study to receive a particular grade. They decide which course is most important and spend more time and energy studying this material. For social functions, students must also budget and distribute their time, energy, and resources. May and June are times of intense social gatherings, at both school and home. Students talk about and plan these events during school time.

Mobilization activities require that students achieve a balance in the time, energy, and resources they commit to each task and social function. Regulating the flow of one's energy so that essential tasks are completed first, and other, less important tasks later, requires a certain degree of maturity on the part of the student. Younger elementary students rarely have the judgmental facilities to make this kind of decision, so during the performing stage the teacher usually budgets and distributes the time, energy, and resources of students. Older students are expected to exercise greater judgment in the use of time, energy, and resources. Some of these students, however, can become overstimulated with the demands of task and social functions and become totally confused as to how to budget and distribute their time and energy appropriately. For example, time and energy needed to study for the social studies final exam is spent planning the school play. These students who have worked hard most of the school year now are faced with the prospect of not being able to successfully complete or perform their course work.

Students are also faced with the eventuality that all things must be completed and end. This disengagement process can vary depending on the grade level you teach. At the upper elementary grade levels—sixth, seventh, eighth—teachers report the month of June as an escalating disengagement from work. At the lower grade levels this process occurs during the last week of school. Cleanup, inventory, final review, makeup tests, year-end picnics and field trips, returning of term papers, notebooks, and workbooks are all activities associated with disengaging. Social/emotional functions tend to be emphasized here. Students feel a sense of unfinished business and hurry to plan summer activities and end-of-school parties. While students are happy the year is over, they report the loss of the accustomed routine and friendships. The teacher who was seen as all-powerful and all-knowing at the beginning of the school year is now seen as a helper and supporter in one's thirst for knowledge. For many students it is difficult to disengage from such a support person.

Characteristics of Task Behavior

- Results are important. Individual preferences are often put aside until the task is completed.
- The teacher is viewed as a resource person rather than as an authority figure.
- More and more insight emerges during class discussions.
- Some individuals complete more than what is required and others show a desire to do something for the rest of the school.
- Differences in support and affection among individual members is tolerated as long as the class task can be accomplished.

Characteristics of Social/Emotional Behavior

- Individuals are allowed to assume new roles or to give up past roles.
- Hostile behavior is accepted as part of the idiosyncratic behavior of individuals.
- Extreme emotional outbursts which draw from class time are not tolerated.
- More and more interdependency among group members is shown.

Management Strategies

1. Act as a facilitator in directing the class to finish its work. Encourage those that are working hard. Help those who are lagging by establishing a time-management system. Break the assignments due down into small tasks and assign due dates for each task.

2. Review and integrate the course material and purpose with future needs of the students. Make them aware of other courses in the school which are related to your course content. Provide summer reading and other activities students can do to enhance their working competence in your course content.

3. Review the class experience during the year. Highlight the events that moved the class as a group from one developmental stage to another. Describe the process in terms of forming, storming, norming, and performing.

4. Allow the class to critique your course curriculum and your teaching style. A questionnaire which can be completed anonymously is appropriate.

5. The use of the exercises which follow this section will help students complete the mobilizing and disengaging activities which are part of this growth stage.

CITY ADVENTURE (PS 1)

Goal

To give students a challenging task, requiring an integration of knowledge gained during the school year.

Procedure

Have the class divide into small groups. Their assignment is to visit three or four places and complete a prearranged task at each site. Explain that the object of the assignment is the successful completion of the agenda before any of the other groups.

Although the sites and the tasks to be performed at each are identical for the groups, the routes the groups eventually take are very different. Each group is responsible for the planning and execution of its agenda. The students must locate the sites, determine the most effective type of transportation to each (based on schedule, costs), calculate expense, and prepare the itinerary.

They should keep secret their final plan. (Note: The students should be reminded that the chaperones are there only for safety measures and to act as timekeepers; the students should not expect the chaperones to offer advice or correct mistakes in their agenda.)

On the day of the trip, start the groups out at the same time, and remind them that in order to successfully complete the assignment all the members of a specific group must stay together. (We suggest that one requirement be to spend a certain amount of time at each site. In that way, students are given an opportunity to enjoy the city.)

Some suggested places to visit in New York City:

Statue of Liberty	Central Park Zoo
Stock Exchange	Civil Court
Lincoln Center	F.A.O. Schwartz's Toy Store
Top of World Trade Center	Shea Stadium
Chinatown	Staten Island Ferry Ride
Museum of Natural History	Rockefeller Center

Some suggested prizes for the winning group:

Free movie tickets	Pizza in school
Lunch at a fast food place	Record album

CLASS PROJECT (PS 2)

Goal

To give students the opportunity to work together and share their skills on a project which helps the school or community.

Procedure

Discuss the reason for a class project stressing the idea of providing service to the school and community. In addition, the students could be told that the project allows other students and teachers in the building to view the class as a productive unit.

The students should brainstorm possible projects. The materials and supplies needed to complete each proposed project should be listed. The teacher should monitor a general discussion on which project is the most likely to succeed with the resources on hand.

The class should vote on the project it will accomplish and assign students to the needed committees. A timetable for completion of the project and the necessary permission needed should be arranged.

Possible suggestions for activities are cleanup of trash along a main street, cleanup of a stream or brook which flows through town, refurbishing a worn town monument, creating a plant display for the principal's office, and so forth.

Money for the projects could be raised through a variety of methods. (A bake sale is a popular activity which allows students to work together and raise some money quickly.)

The students should be encouraged to post a sign or a similar notice that the class is responsible for the project.

BOARD REVIEW (PS 3)

Goal

To help the students review the numerous activities accomplished during the year.

Procedure

Before class, list every possible activity or event that occurred during the school year on the board. We recommend that activities be listed as one word. The words should be spread randomly over the entire board intermixed with descriptive adjectives as shown below. (Colored chalk may make various words stand out.)

Ask each student to connect with chalk two words (one activity word plus one descriptive word). The student must tell the class why he/she feels the words are connectable. (Note: No connecting line can be drawn *through* a word and a word can be used only once.)

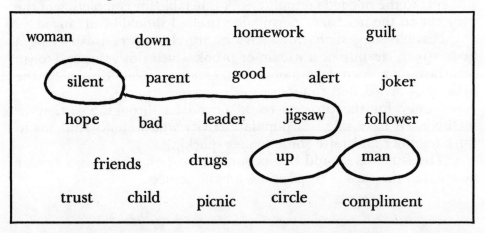

Some of the responses are often quite insightful as can be seen in the board example shown:

"I learned that I can be a man without having to prove it to everyone I meet. Silence is strong."

This activity allows both teacher and students to review the many activities and events offered during the year. This review will be necessary for subsequent activities which have the class evaluate the course. More important, this activity gives the teacher an idea of how certain parts of the course affected certain students.

COURSE EVALUATION (PS 4)

Goal

To help the students evaluate what they liked and disliked about the course.

Procedure

Distribute a copy of the *Final Evaluation* sheet to each student and ask them to fill in the form. Explain that the form will be collected but that no names are required. (The teacher should advise the class that if any students have comments which they are reluctant to share, they may use this time to do so by writing the comments on the sheet.)

After each student has completed the form, ask some students to read what they wrote. We usually find that this activity generates a lot of comments about the course and the teacher. The students feel they have a chance to evaluate, rather than always being evaluated.

You may want to summarize the reactions to the class before the final activity of the month. At the conclusion, collect the forms and use the information in designing the course for the next year.

Figure 1–5 summarizes the stages of class development.

Class Development Stages	Activities for Task and Social/Emotional Functions
1. Forming	Linking Forming Rules and Roles Information Seeking
2. Storming	Distancing Centering
3. Norming	Orienting Fueling
4. Performing	Mobilizing Disengaging

Figure 1–5. *Classroom management review.*

FINAL EVALUATION (PS 4)

Grade _____

Age _____

1. List the one activity you liked the most. Why?

2. List the one activity you liked the least. Why?

3. The most important thing I learned about me this year was _____

_____

_____.

4. The most important thing I learned about life this year was _____

_____

_____.

5. The person who helped me the most in this class was _____.

6. The one thing I would like to see changed or added next year

would be _____

_____.

7. I would recommend this course to others. Why? Why not?

REFERENCES

Bales, Robert F. *Interaction Process Analysis: A Method for the Study of Small Groups.* Chicago: University of Chicago Press, 1950.

Canfield, Jack, and Harold C. Wells. *100 Ways to Enhance Self-Concept in the Classroom.* Englewood Cliffs, New Jersey: Prentice-Hall, 1976.

Everston, Carolyn M; E. T. Emmer; B. S. Clements; J. Sanford; M. E. Worsham, and E. L. Williams. *Organizing and Managing the Elementary School Classroom.* Austin, Texas: The Research and Development Center for Teacher Education, The University of Texas, 1981.

Gibbard, Graham S.; John J. Hartman; and Richard D. Mann, eds. *Analysis of Groups.* San Francisco: Jossey-Bass, 1974.

Goodman, Gay, and R. A. Pendergrass. "Competence in the Management of Classroom Behavior: An Electric Approach," *Education, 96,* Spring 1976, 297–301.

Neilson, Eric H. "Applying a Group Development Model to Managing a Class," *Group Development,* Leland P. Bradford, ed. La Jolla, California: University Associates, 1978.

Shapio, Lawrence. *Games to Grow On: Activities to Help Children Learn Self-Control.* Englewood Cliffs, New Jersey: Prentice-Hall, 1981.

Slavin, Robert E. *Using Student Team Learning.* Baltimore: The Johns Hopkins University Team Learning Project, Center for the Social Organization of Schools, 1980.

Tuckman, Bruce W. "Developmental Sequence in Small Groups," *Psychological Bulletin, 63,* 1965, 384–399.

Discipline Strategies

CHAPTER 2

Discipline is operationally defined as the act of changing student behavior so that the student acts in a more responsible and appropriate manner. The following six techniques have proven to be effective in changing the behavior of disruptive, disaffected, and/or poorly performing students. Each procedure is quite different in its goals, methodology, and appropriateness of use. One may ask, why know six disciplinary procedures when one works just as well? The answer is: not all techniques work all the time with every student. A working knowledge of a number of varied techniques allows you flexibility in meeting both the student's needs and your needs at any given moment. But in cases when a student is very angry and physically or verbally acting out, it is suggested that you turn to Chapter 3, "Confrontation Strategies" and use one of the strategies described.

The techniques discussed in this chapter are arranged on a continuum, as in Figure 2–1. Moving along the continuum, choosing a discipline technique, one finds that the techniques require less and less verbal interaction with the student to produce behavior change. At one pole is active listening—a technique used to engage a student who is highly verbal and who can conceptualize part of the problem. At the other end of the pole is family intervention—a technique used to

Technique	Student Needs
1. Active Listening	<ul><li>expresses many feelings</li><li>wants to talk about problem</li><li>needs some other perspective</li><li>needs to feel accepted</li><li>thoughts and feelings are confused and tends to ramble</li><li>time to work it out</li></ul>
2. Reality Therapy	<ul><li>student wants to talk but needs encouragement and guidance as to content</li><li>behavior needs to be changed</li><li>needs to learn how to take responsibility for behavior</li><li>needs to feel accepted</li><li>can work out a plan to change</li></ul>
3. Assertive Behavior	<ul><li>student's behavior needs to be changed</li><li>refuses to listen to other explanations</li><li>needs to be aware of teacher's rights</li><li>can verbally interact but only to argue</li></ul>
4. Behavior Modification	<ul><li>cannot talk meaningfully about the problem</li><li>refuses to change maladaptive behavior</li><li>needs or desires what teacher has to offer</li><li>can be taught more appropriate behavior</li></ul>
5. Group Contingency Contracting	<ul><li>generally, whole class needs to change its behavior</li><li>peer pressure can influence an individual's behavior</li></ul>
6. Family Intervention	<ul><li>when all the techniques above fail to change behavior</li><li>when siblings have discipline problems as well</li><li>when student cannot determine what is needed or wanted</li><li>when parents state they cannot control their child</li></ul>

Figure 2–1. *Comparison chart of discipline techniques and student needs.*

change the behavior of a student who refuses to talk or change the disruptive behavior. It is essential that the teacher determine the student's needs and be aware of his/her own needs before choosing a particular technique. An attempt to use an active listening technique with a physically aggressive student who will not talk is doomed to failure.

The first two techniques, active listening and reality therapy, are preferable to the latter ones in that they allow students to become verbally involved in the change process and take more responsibility for the change. However, it is clear that not all students will respond to these first two techniques, in which case more structural procedures would be called for.

As far as the teacher's needs are concerned, it is our experience that the most successful implementation of a discipline procedure is one in which the teacher considers the following points:

1. What do you want to happen as a result of this effort?
2. When is the best time and where is the best place for this to occur?
3. What do you anticipate the student's response to be?
4. How will you deal with this response?
5. Is there room for negotiation in your desired objective?
6. What is your plan or procedure, should the original plan not work?

Finally, it should be pointed out that each technique, regardless of how much verbal interaction is required, also requires that a teacher show care and concern for the student. The student must feel that the teacher believes in him/her, sees some good, and cares enough to try if the student is going to cooperate. Without this human involvement, the technique described will appear to be insensitive and mechanical.

ACTIVE LISTENING

Active listening (Gordon 1974) is the attempt by the teacher to help the student understand the words and feelings behind their statements; to help them clarify the problem, propose solutions, and change inappropriate behavior. The teacher will need a deep sense of trust in the student's ability to solve his/her own problems and must be willing to spend time with the student talking about and listening to the student's concerns. The teacher must be willing to share his/her own feelings about the situation.

When to Use

Active listening is appropriate to use with a student who is very verbal and wants to talk the problem out. It demands time, so if a teacher is looking for an immediate behavior change, this technique may not be the first choice. But, the technique does help the teacher build a strong positive relationship with the student which should be transferrable to other problems in the future. It is an excellent technique to use with a student who says a lot but tends to ramble and becomes unfocused as to where the problem rests.

Procedures

Active listening can be divided into three major phases with specific core conditions to be established in each (Carkhuff et al 1968). Behavior change, it should be noted, occurs primarily in the third phase.

Phase I:
Building a Relationship

The goal of this phase is to establish a strong rapport with the student by communicating to the student that you have listened and understood the problem. You may not agree with the student's behavior, but you have tried to understand the reasons for it. The three core conditions needed to be established here are as follows:

Empathy: the ability to see the student's problems and concerns through his/her eyes; i.e., a "feeling with" as opposed to sympathy, which is "feeling like."

Respect: belief in the student's worth and potential; a nonjudgmental acceptance of a student.

Warmth: a caring and concern for the student that is evident.

Research in counseling indicates that if the listener gives at least three empathetic responses to the speaker's statement *before* offering advice, asking questions, or interpreting feelings, there is a significantly greater chance that the student will trust the listener more, listen to the advice, and return. As adults, many teachers presume they know what the student's problem is and how to go about solving it even before the student has had an opportunity to explain the whole situation. Usually, the teacher does know the problem and solution, based on years of experience with similar situations. However, it is unwise to rush in and give advice, interpret, or ask questions before the student finishes expressing his/her feelings. Remember, the student needs to know you have listened to the unique problem.

There are two techniques to use to convey to the student that you have listened and have tried to understand. The first is listening for the content of the statement and simply rephrasing the content back to the student. Two examples:

STUDENT: I couldn't get my homework done last night because of the game.

TEACHER: You couldn't get the homework done because of the game.

STUDENT: Why do I get caught all the time? Others cut and they don't get caught.

TEACHER: You are wondering why you get caught and others don't.

At first glance you may say that no student will allow you to repeat every word they say like a "dumb tape recorder." Generally speaking, students are not aware that you are repeating their content. The typical student response to both of these examples is, "Yeah," a recognition that you have captured the essence of what was said. What they do hear is you listening.

The second technique for building the core conditions of empathy, respect, and warmth is listening for feelings and stating these feelings to the student. For example:

STUDENT: I came late to class because Paul hid my books, the bum.

TEACHER: You are angry with him.

STUDENT: Why do I fail all the time? Others don't study and they don't fail.

TEACHER: You are pretty angry about failing all the time.

The teacher in both these cases is taking an educated guess as to the feelings behind the student's statement. Often the voice tone or how words are pronounced reveal feelings. Don't be afraid to guess at the feeling. The student will correct you if you are wrong. Regardless, the student's feeling has been clarified.

Again, three responses using listening for content and listening for feeling move the teacher to the next phase.

Phase II:
Defining the Problem

The goal of this phase is to help the student view the problem with clarity and specificity. Three core conditions need to be established:

Concreteness: The teacher can recognize vagueness and clarity in a student's statements. The teacher is clear about what is expected.

Genuineness: The teacher is honest with his or her own feelings which serve as a model for the student.

Self-Disclosure: The teacher volunteers experiences and feelings similar to those of the student.

There are three methods of being concrete and genuine with a student. The first is to use "I" statements. For example:

TEACHER: I think the problem is greater than losing a boyfriend.
TEACHER: I feel a bit concerned here also.
TEACHER: I still want you to be on time, so I guess we have a conflict.

To be more specific, if you want to be concrete and genuine with the student, state what you feel and think about his/her view of the problem. Get the student to do the same by making "I" statements. Ask the student to state what part of the problem is fuzzy and needs more clarifying.

A second method is to summarize all the difficulties and positive resources (if there are any) which encompass the student's problem. For example:

TEACHER: You mentioned you were failing English, social studies, and health, that you like your English and health teachers, but could probably pass social studies with some after-school help from a teacher you hate.

Summarizing is like taking all the verbiage the student has been delivering and funneling it down to certain core issues or problems. It saves the student from rambling and helps you get on with the task of helping the student.

A third method is to prioritize the problems for the student by asking the student which problem or aspect of it should be addressed first. For example:

> TEACHER: Which subject—English, social studies, or health—do you want to start improving first?

Many students want to tackle all their problems at once. This usually meets with total failure just from the sheer volume of the task. By helping a student prioritize, you are helping the student solve each problem one at a time before moving on to the next. Consequently, the task does not seem so overwhelming to the student.

Self-disclosure is a tricky business. You should avoid giving the student the impression you have been through it all. Remember, most students see themselves and their problems as unique. They are skeptical of one who says, "I know exactly what you are going through. When I was thirteen years old the same thing happened to me." Use self-disclosure only if you feel a student would trust you more if he/she knew more about you as a person rather than as a teacher.

Phase III:
Problem Solving

The goal of this final phase is to have the student develop solutions to the problems being discussed. The core conditions needed are:

Confrontation: The ability of the teacher to illustrate a discrepancy between what a student says and what he/she does.

Immediacy: The teacher focuses on the present and immediate interactions with the student.

Remember, during this phase you want to see some action, some movement toward solving the problem. The three procedures to use are brainstorming, decision making, and implementation steps.

Ask the student to brainstorm as many different solutions to the problem as he/she can think of.

Next, ask the student to decide which solutions are possible, which can be agreed to by both student and teacher, and which can be completed in a relatively short time. Once a decision has been made on one solution, have the student develop a time plan for implementation—who will do what when.

During these three procedures the teacher should be pointing out discrepancies between what a student says and what he wants to do. An example of a student who is always tardy:

STUDENT: I just cannot think of any solutions to this problem. I need your class but I can't seem to get to first period in time. There are problems to everything I think of.

TEACHER: You said earlier [during Phase II: Being Concrete] that you wanted to pass this course and not be dropped. Now you are telling me that you can't think of even one solution to solve your problem. Which is it going to be?

Also, the teacher should be immediate with the student.

TEACHER: Mark, I admire how you have tried to work through this problem. You have talked it out with me, seem to trust me, and I feel you really want to get things fixed up.

Another example:

TEACHER: Mark, I am confused now about how to handle your indecision. On the one hand, you say you want to change, but I don't see any change. I am becoming annoyed at your lack of progress.

During Phase III you will need to make use of "I" statements and reflect content and feeling statements in order to keep the student moving toward a problem solution. As you can see from these examples, you are very involved in the student's change process. You not only develop feelings about what is going on, but you communicate these feelings to the student in a clear, caring manner.

The following example of a student-teacher dialogue illustrates the various phases and core conditions which comprise the active listening behavior change technique. The example is of a seventh-grader who has not completed her homework for one week.

TEACHER: Sue, I need to talk to you about not having any homework from you this week.   (Teacher uses "I" statements to be very clear.)

STUDENT: Well, I know I should bring it in but there is so much going on.

                                                  <u>Phase I</u>

TEACHER: You said there is so much going on?   (Reflection of content.)

STUDENT:	Yeah, my brother is home from college and he has my room. I have no place to do my work, no place for anything.	(Student recognizes that the teacher has heard her by saying, "Yeah.")
TEACHER:	Your brother is home from college and you have no place to put things. You seem angry at losing your room.	(Reflection of content twice and reflection of feeling once.)
STUDENT:	Very angry is the word for it. My mother just gave my room away without asking!	(Student validates teacher's recognition of angry feeling.)
TEACHER:	You are angry with your mother also.	(Reflection of feeling.)
STUDENT:	I am angry with both of them.	

Phase II

TEACHER:	Well, the way I see it, you have a problem. You have no place to do your homework, you are angry, and your teacher is demanding work from you. I can see your dilemma and respect it.	(Teacher is concrete and genuine with student by summarizing the problem and making an "I" statement about how she feels.)
STUDENT:	I don't know how to deal with all this.	(Student is making "I" statement and expressing a need to be more clear; student is expressing a genuine confusion.)
TEACHER:	Let's deal with the homework issue first. I need your homework and you say you have no place to do it.	(Teacher is concrete and limits discussion to one aspect of the problem by prioritizing. She defines the two positions very clearly.)
STUDENT:	Okay, what can I do?	

Phase III

TEACHER:	Let's think of some alternative places you can get your work done.	(Teacher suggests brainstorming solutions.)

STUDENT:	Yeah...I suppose I could stop at the library on my way home and do it.	
TEACHER:	I like that idea. Can you see any problems with it?	(Teacher is immediate and expresses feelings.)
STUDENT:	Well, it is out of my way, I would rather do my work at night, and sometimes my friends bother me on the way to the library.	
TEACHER:	What I hear are more inconveniences than real problems. If you really want to change, some inconvenience is necessary. Is any other place better?	(Teacher confronts discrepancy between what student says she wants and the minor excuses she gives for not doing work at the library. Then teacher asks her to brainstorm more.)
STUDENT:	No, not really. Well, okay, I'll try the library.	(Student does not need to brainstorm and completes Phase III with a plan to change.)
TEACHER:	I am pleased with how you handled this problem and came up with a solution. Perhaps at some other time we could talk about what is happening at home.	(Teacher is immediate, honest, and clear with feelings.)

Figure 2–2 summarizes the phases of active listening.

REALITY THERAPY

This behavior change technique is very specific, as it focuses on the student's behavior, responsibility for behavior, and ways of changing that behavior (Glasser 1965). While it does not ignore student feelings, neither does it encourage the teacher to talk about them. Often students may talk at length about the feelings surrounding an issue and still produce no behavior change. Teaching students to assume responsibility for their behavior is the goal of this technique. It is expected that as students assume responsibility for their behavior, they will start behaving more appropriately. The methodology used is a form of active questioning in which the teacher first has the student

	Core Conditions	Procedures
Phase I Building a relationship	Empathy Respect Warmth	Use three reflections of content and feelings statements.
Phase II Defining the problem	Concreteness Genuineness Self-Disclosure	Use "I" statements, summarize, prioritize, share your own experiences
Phase III Problem Solving	Confrontation Immediacy	Use brainstorming, decision making, implementation steps; point out discrepancies between what is said and what is done.

Figure 2–2. *Active listening review.**

evaluate the behavior, and then choose an action plan to change irresponsible behavior.

When to Use

This technique is appropriate to use with students who cannot understand and do not wish to talk about their feelings. Students involved in this procedure should be able to trust the teacher, at least minimally, and to view the teacher as someone who can help. Students should be able to verbally engage the teacher.

Procedure

Reality therapy can best be described as a series of questions. You start by having the student describe the behavior, evaluate it, decide to change it, and develop an action plan to change it. The questions are relatively straightforward. If a student gets stuck at one point, you just recycle the questions.

1. *What Are You Doing?* Here, you want the student to talk about what he/she has done. You may know it and the student may know it, but by having the student describe the situation, problem, or behavior, you are

*Taken from Lawrence M. Brammer, *The Helping Relationship, Process and Skills* (Englewood Cliffs, N.J.: Prentice-Hall, Inc., 1973), p. 79.

bringing the event into the student's consciousness. All of the specific behaviors are brought out, because eventually what needs to be changed will be found in these specifics. Here is an example of a resistant student:

TEACHER: What happened in class today?

STUDENT: Nothing.

TEACHER: Nothing? How come I saw you standing over that tipped desk?

STUDENT: Oh that. Well, the desk tipped and I stood up just in time to avoid it.

TEACHER: Did the desk fall over by itself?

STUDENT: Mike gave it a shove and it went over.

TEACHER: Show me how Mike gave it a shove.

STUDENT: Like this [he demonstrates].

TEACHER: I see. And what were you doing when Mike had his hand on your desk?

STUDENT: Nothing...trying to get away from his fingers.

TEACHER: Did you get away? Show me what you were doing.

STUDENT: I was leaning like this. Mike was trying to grab his pen back and wham, over it went.

TEACHER: You had his pen. How did that happen?

STUDENT: I took it as a joke. I was going to give it back.

TEACHER: This is what happened. You took Mike's pen, he leaned over to get it back, and your desk fell over in the process.

STUDENT: Yeah.

2. *How Did It Help You?* Ask the student if what was done was good or bad for him or her. Ask if the action helped now, not when it was done. Have the student, not you, make an evaluation of his/her behavior. If you say, "That was bad," you are evaluating the student's behavior and thereby depriving the student of the need to take responsibility for his/her own actions. Remember, students will do things that give them pleasure. If an action can be seen as hurting them or getting them into conflict with you, they will avoid it. Many students do things for you, including behaving well, because they want to please you. By pleasing you they are pleasing themselves. Continuing our dialogue with the student:

TEACHER: How did the desk falling over help you?

STUDENT: It was funny. Everyone laughed.

TEACHER: Yes, they did. But now you have to see me after school and I will need to write a referral on you. How does the desk falling over help you now?

STUDENT: I guess not much.

3. *Can We Develop a Plan to Change?* At this point, you do not ask if the student wants to change. You imply that change is necessary. You also imply that you are willing to work with the student to develop a plan. Your involvement is critical if the student's behavior is going to change. Ask the student for any ideas about how to get out of the mess he/she is in. Ask if the student knows anyone who has a similar problem. In making a plan, have the student be as specific as possible. Who is going to do what and when? Be careful not to take too much responsibility and end up giving so much advice that you develop the plan, rather than the student. Often, if the student follows your advice and it fails, the student will come back complaining that *your* plan failed and *you* really have gotten him/her in more trouble. Part of having the student develop responsibility is to have him/her develop an individual plan to change inappropriate behavior. For example:

TEACHER: Can we make a plan to change?

STUDENT: What do you want me to do?

TEACHER: What can you do to fix this mess up?

STUDENT: I could apologize to you and the class.

TEACHER: How would that help?

STUDENT: I don't know. It would be a start.

TEACHER: What else could be done?

STUDENT: I could leave Mike alone in class.

TEACHER: How are you going to do that?

STUDENT: I'll sit across the room. I won't even see him.

TEACHER: I hear you with two plans. One is to apologize to me and the class. The second is to move to the other side of the room. Do you want to do both?

STUDENT: Sure.

TEACHER: All right, let's get down to specifics. When are you going to apologize?

STUDENT: Tomorrow's class.

TEACHER: What time?

STUDENT: In the morning sometime.

TEACHER: What time in the morning?

STUDENT: Okay, at 9:30 A.M.

TEACHER: How are you going to do it?

STUDENT: I'll stand up in front of the class and say something.

TEACHER: What are you going to say?

STUDENT: I'm sorry teacher and class for causing my desk to be tipped over.

TEACHER: Okay, now about moving away from Mike?

STUDENT: I'll do it tomorrow, first thing.

4. *Can We Make a Contract?* Here the teacher summarizes the plan for the student. Adolescents do not like written plans, but for younger children simple written plans work well. For adolescents, a verbal agreement is sufficient. A contract influences behavior. Get involved in the contract by specifying what you will do. For example, the student can call you or report after school to briefly tell you how his/her plan for change worked. Your side of the contract shows the student you care and also puts pressure on him/her to fulfill the agreement. For example:

TEACHER: Then I presume we have a contract here.

STUDENT: Yeah.

TEACHER: To summarize, you are going to stand up in front of the class at 9:30 A.M. tomorrow and say you are sorry to me and to the other students that you caused the desk to be tipped. You also will move your desk to the other side of the room first thing in the morning.

STUDENT: That's what I'll do.

TEACHER: For my sake, I will not write a referral on you and I see no point in calling your parents.* At the end of class let's talk briefly and see how it went, okay?

STUDENT: Okay.

5. *Follow-Up.* Very often even the best of plans fails. In fact, for a student who has been failing or misbehaving over a long period of time, failure can be expected. It is what they do best. Do not listen to excuses for failure because to do so is to tell the student that you accept these

---

*Often a student does something that necessitates following the natural consequences. If a student hit another, for example, the teacher in most schools would have to report it regardless of the student's plan. Here, however, the teacher could exercise her own judgment.

excuses. Don't punish the student for failing and don't give up. The best procedure is to recycle the questions. For example:

TEACHER: What happened with your plan?
STUDENT: I forgot at 9:30 A.M.
TEACHER: How did forgetting help you?
STUDENT: It didn't. I guess I still have to do it.
TEACHER: Can we make a plan to help you remember?
STUDENT: Sure, how about I set my watch alarm to go off?
TEACHER: Okay, let's try that tomorrow at 9:30 A.M.

No-Nos

When implementing reality therapy, there are a few things you should not do.

1. *Do not deal with feelings.* Feelings are dead ends. Students often do not know why they do things. If they do tell you their feelings, you enter their subjective world where you cannot win unless you are willing to engage in a long conversation. If a student tells you your class is boring and that is why he is always late, you will find yourself arguing about his feelings of boredom rather than the fact that he is breaking one of your class rules and is acting irresponsibly. Recognize feelings, but do not talk about them. Talk about behavior.

2. *Do not ask the question, "Why?"* This question often leads to feeling-type responses. For example, "I hate him," "I felt like it," "I'm depressed." Even if you know why and if it was an accurate diagnosis, there is little chance it could help you in getting a student to change inappropriate behavior. Another reason for not asking why is that often a student does not know why.

3. *Do not talk about the past or the future.* Events in the past cannot be changed. Events in the future often are talked about like magical thinking. For example, a student would often say that if only he/she had a certain teacher then he/she would not fail. This may or may not be true, but it is often outside the realm of possibilities in which you are dealing. Talk about the present with the student. What is he/she doing now and how is it helping now? It is hardest for a student to accept responsibility for the present.

4. *Do not accept failure.* You will need patience to deal with students who have chronic histories of failing and acting inappropriately. When

they fail they expect you to get mad at them; this is what they expect from those in authority, and failing is what they do best. If a student fails in not fulfilling the contract, recycle the questions: "What did you do?" and "How did failing help you?" and "Can we make a plan not to fail?"

Following is an illustration of reality therapy. An eleven-year-old boy is referred to his teacher for being in the bathroom without a pass rather than in class. This is the second incident. Figure 2-3 summarizes reality therapy.

TEACHER:	Mike, can you tell me what happened today?	(Teacher asks first question even though they both know what happened. The question has to be asked twice.)
STUDENT:	Nothing really.	
TEACHER:	Well, what did you do or not do that the assistant principal had to bring you back to class?	
STUDENT:	He told you. I was in the bathroom. I wasn't doing anything.	
TEACHER:	He said you were sitting on the sink. You were supposed to be in my class.	(Teacher supplies facts to help student describe the event.)
STUDENT:	So what?	
TEACHER:	How did it help you?	(Teacher asks second question, helping the student to evaluate his behavior.)
STUDENT:	I got out of class and had a smoke.	
TEACHER:	Yes, but how is it helping you now?	(Teacher avoids talking about the past and about student's failings.)
STUDENT:	You mean now?	
TEACHER:	You were skipping class and now you have to see me about it. How does that help you now?	(Teacher makes the evaluation occur in the present, not when the event happened.)
STUDENT:	At the time it was fine.	
TEACHER:	And now?	

STUDENT:	It could be better!	
TEACHER:	Can we make a plan to change your habit of skipping my class?	(Teacher asks third question.)
STUDENT:	I want to stay in your room.	
TEACHER:	Can't we think of things that you could do to make sure you get to my class?	(Teacher asks student to be specific.)
STUDENT:	Well, I guess I could come right into the room at the beginning of the period.	
TEACHER:	Anything else you can think of?	(More specifics are asked for.)
STUDENT:	I'll ask for a pass to the bathroom. You do have passes?	
TEACHER:	All right. You mentioned two things you could do. One is to come to the room right after your prior class and the second is to ask me for a pass to the bathroom.	(Teacher summarizes.)
	Yes, I do have passes. I presume you would like to establish a contract for tomorrow which states what you are going to do and when.	(Teacher moves to fourth question. It is obvious the student wants to make an agreement.)
STUDENT:	Okay.	
TEACHER:	And at the end of class tomorrow let's review the contract.	(Teacher prepares for a follow-up.)

Key Questions	No-Nos
1. What are you doing?	Feelings
2. How is it helping you?	The question "Why?"
3. Can we make a plan to change?	The past or future
4. Can we make a contract?	Accepting failure
5. Follow-up.	

Figure 2–3. *Reality therapy review.*

ASSERTIVE BEHAVIOR

The goal of this technique is to change student behavior with as little verbal interaction as possible. The teacher's directives are perceived as clear, determined, and uncompromising. A student who has used aggressive behavior or the threat of it or verbal games in order to intimidate and manipulate a teacher to cede to his/her demands will find that a teacher using assertive behavior is operating from a position of strength. Experience has demonstrated that teachers who have assertive skills can employ these skills to manage a student or a class of students without "losing their cool" or becoming aggressive themselves (throwing chalk or yelling at a student). Assertive skills are easy to understand and to learn, and they can be incorporated into any classroom situation.

When to Use

If a student refuses to talk to you about changing inappropriate behavior by being verbally defensive, sullen, or withdrawn, any extensive verbal discipline technique would probably not be effective. Very often a student needs to know what you want, how you want it done, and how determined you are to get it. The techniques you will learn in this chapter deliver a concise, clear message. Also, there are times you need to demand behavior change immediately, and don't have time to engage students in active listening or reality therapy techniques. A simple directive, delivered in an uncompromising manner, is often enough to get students on task.

Assertive Rights

1. Always have a mind-set that operates from strength rather than weakness. Believe in yourself and the statement, "Can do." Some students will try to intimidate you; others will say they don't understand you.

2. If an event is over, don't talk about it.

3. Perseverance pays off.

4. You never win if you need to prove you are the winner.

5. Never expect students to understand what you are feeling or thinking.

6. Never argue. Arguing with a student implies the other is right.

7. Never feel guilty about being assertive. Others will try to make you feel awkward or guilty.

8. You have a right to have a "bad" day; to make a mistake in your classroom performance; to not know something.

9. You have a right to say to a student, "Not today, try me tomorrow," "I don't care," "Because I said so," and "Give me a break today."

Procedure

Five Nonverbal Assertive Behaviors. The following nonverbal behaviors are important to maintain as they communicate your determination to change a student's disruptive or poor behavior.

1. *The head* should be positioned directly in front of the person being addressed, with the chip up.

2. *The eyes* should be directed at the person being addressed. Focus and maintain eye contact while you speak.

3. *The voice* should be clear and firm, conveying your message in as few sentences as possible. Never ramble on about what you want. The person you are addressing should be able to remember exactly what you are requesting. A loud voice is not necessary; a firm, clear tone is more effective.

4. *The arms and hands* should be positioned at your sides or in front of you as you speak, generating an impression of openness. Never cross your arms on your chest or put your hands on your hips; this posture conveys an offensive stance. The hands should not be clenched, as this position also conveys an aggressive message.

5. *The legs and feet* should be positioned in front of the person addressed. Be careful not to stand with the legs and feet too far apart, as this position conveys an aggressive message.

The following nonverbal behaviors should be avoided:

- scratching, rubbing, or shifting the body
- playing with your hair, beard, jewelry, pen, or clothing
- pacing
- putting your hands up to your face

Four Verbal Assertive Behaviors. The following techniques are examples of what to say when you want to assert yourself—and how to say it.

1. *Stating a Demand:* This technique has four components:

State what you saw. (Use behavioral terms.)
State your need. (Use a feeling word.)
State your reason. (Start with "Because....")
State your demand. (Describe specific behavior.)

Example:

TEACHER:	I saw you talking with Anthony.	(States what was seen.)
	I am bothered by it, because it disturbs me and him.	(Need expressed with use of a feeling word. States reason.)
	I want you to be quiet now.	(States what you want to happen.)

2. *Persistence:* This technique is excellent in those situations in which a student is trying to get you to do something against your wishes, is saying he/she won't do something, or is ignoring your legitimate request. By simply, quietly, but firmly repeating your request, you can show the student you are determined to have your needs met. An example follows:

TEACHER: I want you to stop coming to my class late.
STUDENT: Aw...you know how hard it is to get here from gym.
TEACHER: I know it is a long trip, but others make it. I want you to stop coming to my class late.
STUDENT: It's too hard.
TEACHER: I want you to stop coming to my class late.

As you read this example, you probably are saying that this technique is nothing new to you. You are right. You can hear this "persistence" technique every day in most school buildings. Being aware of its existence is crucial for you. It provides you with another strategy to change student behavior.

3. *Reframing:* This technique allows you to take a student's negative verbal statement and turn it around by providing a positive perspective to the matter. This technique is not a simple play on words, as that would be unfair and demeaning to a student. Rather, it is an honest attempt to provide the student with a different view of the problem. Once a student

has this alternative perspective, it is possible that consequently his/her behavior will change. Example:

STUDENT: This class is boring; everyone sleeps here.

TEACHER: How observant you are to notice everyone sleeping. You must be awake.

STUDENT: Huh? You are boring.

TEACHER: Again, you show remarkable observation and evaluation skills to make a judgment of this type.

STUDENT: What about the boring?

TEACHER: You are awake enough to make an observation and make a statement based on those facts.

4. *Negotiating:* Most students will work out a compromise with you if their basic rights are not violated. Most teachers can participate in a compromise as long as the class rules and their own rights are not violated. A compromise can be an effective solution. Often, it can be initiated by simply saying, "Can you and I work out some sort of compromise on this?" Example:

STUDENT: I would like to go to the library this period.

TEACHER: I would like you to use the library also. However, if you recall the last time you went to the library, you stayed beyond the class period. I had to come and get you.

STUDENT: That won't happen again.

TEACHER: It had better not. Can we compromise on this issue? I want you to use the library and you want to use the library. Is that correct?

STUDENT: Yes.

TEACHER: And I want you back on time and you say you want to be back on time. Right?

STUDENT: Right.

TEACHER: Okay, in order to compromise on this, I want you to go to the library and come back in twenty minutes. That is, at 1:20 P.M. I would like you back here. Is that acceptable?

STUDENT: Why not the whole period?

TEACHER: Because I first want to see if you can handle twenty minutes at the library and get back here on time. If you can do this then I'll extend the privilege for the full forty minutes. This way you get what you want—to use the library—and I get what I want—you back on time.

Linguistics

Changing your language can help you express your needs in a clear, concise, and honest manner. As a result, the message that comes across is a strong one.

"I" statements

Change "it" to "I":
It bothers me to hear you say that.
(I feel bothered when you say that.)

Change "you" to "I":
You are always doing this to me.
(I feel you are always doing this to me.)

Change "we" to "I":
We all like to do art.
(I enjoy having everyone do art.)

Verb statements

Change "can't" to "won't":
I can't stand this anymore.
(I won't stand this anymore.)

Change "need" to "want":
I need to have all the homework in.
(I want to have all the homework in.)

Change "have to" to "choose to":
I have to suspend you.
(I choose to suspend you.)

Reaffirming Purpose

Often students forget why they are working on a certain project, why they are in school, or why they have to work with you. A simple reminder of the purpose is enough to motivate them to get back on task. The teacher asks the class to open their books and start working on problem number 16. While the rest of the class is working on the assignment, the teacher notices that Billy is just staring at her. Billy has refused to do class assignments in the past. The teacher simply stands over Billy, maintaining direct eye contact, and says in a firm voice, "I expect you to do it now" or "Do it now" or "You are taking this course for credit, aren't you?"

Time Limit

Many students work best under pressure; others need to be reminded that a project does not take all day. A reminder that you have a time limit often gets the task done faster. If a class is working too slowly on a project or problem and many students are talking instead of working, the teacher might say firmly, "You have six more minutes, and then I want it."

Guilt Reverse

Students can blame you for problems associated with their failure to obey the rules. Also, when you remind them of the rules, they can become angry at you. They try to give you the feeling that the rules are a violation of their rights. In cases like this, reverse the guilt they are trying to dump on you. If a student is refusing to obey a teacher's request to leave the halls or bathroom, the teacher can defuse the situation and reverse the responsibility of the student's behavior: "Don't give me any more grief today. I've had my share of it. Why are you doing this to me?"

Figure 2–4 on page 70 summarizes assertive behavior.

BEHAVIOR MODIFICATION

Behavior modification is a form of discipline that focuses primarily on what a student does, not on what he or she thinks or feels. The basic premise of this method is that individuals engage in behavior that rewards them. The process of behavior change involves changing the reward system so that new behavior is established and unwanted behavior is eliminated. Using contingency contracting, the teacher offers simple rewards if and when a student shows some change. Once the unwanted behavior is no longer present, the rewards can be withdrawn gradually so the new behavior is evident on its own. The mechanism for this change process involves little verbal interaction, but it does involve a contract between the teacher and student. The rewards need not be material add-ons, but social privileges the student already has access to. Tell the student he/she must give to get.

Nonverbal Assertive Behaviors

1. Head position
2. Eye contact
3. Voice
4. Arms and hands
5. Legs and feet
(Avoid shifting and fidgeting with objects.)

Verbal Assertive Behaviors

1. Stating a demand
2. Persistence
3. Reframing
4. Negotiating

Linguistics
"I" Statements
Verb Statements

Reaffirming Purpose

Time Limit

Guilt Reverse

Figure 2–4. *Assertive behavior review.*

When to Use

This technique is appropriate to use with students who have shown little interest in taking more responsibility for their behavior. It is useful for those students who need a structure for behavior change imposed. Students are encouraged to become part of the change process by helping the teacher negotiate a contract. If, however, meaningful talk with a student about a problem is impossible, then the structure for change is initiated by the teacher. It is desirable for students to want something from the teacher (grades, praise, rewards) or from the school (registration, diploma, a place to be) for this technique to work. This desire may be only at a primitive level, but it must be there.

Procedure

There are five stages to completing a successful contract for behavior modification.

1. Select an observable behavior that can be changed. Label this behavior in concrete terms. For example, a student is not "disruptive" but "shouts" or "gets out of his seat."
2. Observe the behavior to establish a baseline or a recording of how often it happens. For example, "John, you have missed homework for three out of the past five nights."
3. Negotiate with the student about the observed behavior, the reason for change, and the rewards to be obtained. For example, you may mention to the student that homework is counted in the final grade, that he has missed three-fifths of the assignments, and that he must now stay after school in detention to complete missed work.
4. Establish a contract, either written or verbal, that both can agree on. It is best to be as specific as possible in the language of the contract. For example, "Okay, John, for every day you come to school without homework you will spend 40 minutes in after-school detention to complete missed work."
5. Always determine a date to rewrite or renegotiate the contract. You may need to tighten it up or even relax it, depending on the student's progress. The date also tells the student that there is an end to this process and therefore makes the change less insurmountable. For example, say, "Let's meet next Friday afternoon to see how you are doing."

Rewards for students must be both age-appropriate and not worth a great deal of money. There are three types of rewards:

1. *Tokens:* These are chips, marbles, stars, or points given after the student completes a contractual agreement. They may be redeemed

for smaller prizes, or accumulated for the "purchase" of larger items.

2. *Materials:* These are things such as edible treats or recreational items. Students can supply you with a list of materials they feel are exciting enough.

3. *Social:* Teacher attention and praise, or the opportunity to do a task for the teacher are rewards that are often sufficient to satisfy a student's needs.

Four Sample Behavior Modification Programs

These four programs vary in complexity. While they are oriented toward the elementary grade level, the particular design of the program will have to be adjusted to meet your own needs and the needs of your students.

Program One. Each day students are given from one to twenty points based on work completed and behavior. For example, a completed workbook assignment is worth ten points; being silent in line going to lunch is worth five points; not gettting out of your seat during reading is worth three points. At the end of the day each student is told their total cumulative points. On Friday afternoons the teacher opens the school store. Here students can "purchase" various items for the points earned. The items are typical high interest things like comic books, pencils, small plastic animals, pictures, fruit, and so forth. All the items are donated by the parents at the beginning of the year. Students can serve as accountants, bankers, and store managers.

Program Two. A teacher discussed with John the problem of his not turning in homework. The teacher reported that John had missed homework three out of five nights. She confronted John with her data and discussed with him the need for a behavior modification schedule. They both agreed to the program. John signed a contract that he would complete half of his homework each night for five nights. As a reward, the teacher allowed John to accumulate points (one for each night) which could be used to "purchase" french fries in the school cafeteria. A box of french fries cost John five points. Points were awarded on a daily basis when John turned in his homework. John also kept a graph to plot the number of days and points he accumulated. The first week of the program was so successful that the teacher decided during the second week John would have to complete *all* his homework each night to receive his one point. At the end of four weeks John had not missed homework one night and the program was withdrawn by mutual consent of the teacher and John. The reason only half of the homework was required the first week was to allow John to at least start the process of doing his work without feeling overwhelmed. The french fries were a minor expense for the teacher as she negotiated a cheap price (10¢ a box) from the cafeteria manager.

Program Three. This is an eight-week or a quarterly schedule of reinforcement to help increase academic work and positive behavior. At the end of each week the teacher reports to each student his/her grade for the week. The student receives an "average" grade for the eight weeks on the quarterly report card.

1. *Attendance* (one-third of the grade)
   A—two days or less missed
   B—three to four days missed
   C—four to five days missed
   D—six days missed
   F—over six days missed

2. *Class work* (one-third of the grade)
   Homework
   Participation
   Quizzes

3. *Behavior* (one-third of the grade)
   A—no discipline referrals
   B—one discipline referral
   C—two discipline referrals
   D—three discipline referrals
   F—three or more discipline referrals or a school suspension

Program Four. This program is comprehensive in that it covers most student behavior, academic and social, during the course of a day. Every student in this class is on such a program and everything the teacher gives as part of the program is considered a privilege in this class. Points are needed for field trips, concerts, recess, use of the gym during lunch, breaks, snacks, use of the game room, transfer to another program, and supply items. The teacher keeps the "books" on the students' cumulative points and posts the progress of each student on the class bulletin board.

Class Rules

Each student is rated a 0, 1, or 2 on each of the seven criteria behaviors listed below. If a student does a good job in adhering to this behavior, a 2 is given. If only moderate compliance to the behavior was seen, the teacher gives a 1. If there is no evidence of this behavior, a 0 is given. Checkout time for each student occurs at the end of the school day. If a student or the entire class goes to another teacher's class (physical education, music, art, or shop), they also receive a rating from that teacher. A sample checkout chart is provided in Figure 2–5. Note there is room for point totals as well as for point deductions, depending on whether the student is penalized or purchases an item with points accumulated. Simple items such as paper, pencils, food, toys, games, and so forth, that you can gather from the principal, parents, or students themselves can be used.

1. Comes to class on time and is prepared
2. Completes assigned work
3. Follows teacher directions
4. Appropriate verbal behavior
5. Hall conduct (must have a pass)
6. Handles material appropriately
7. On task behavior (at desk)

Class Levels

The students can earn their right to occupy three different levels of privileges according to how well they perform on the seven criteria behaviors. Each level has its own privileges with specific minimum requirements to complete each day to stay on the level and to advance to the next level.

Level I

- Two bathroom privileges a day
- No recess allowed
- Lunch must be eaten in the classroom
- No extra snack items allowed

Time—must pass five consecutive days
Passing standard—a minimum of three 2s

Level II

- Unlimited bathroom privileges but a pass from the teacher is needed

TEACHER: _____ CLASS: _____ DATE: _____

ATTENDANCE:		(0, 1, or 2 Earned Points)														Adjustments				
Absent _____ Susp'd _____ Note: Asterisked (-X-) behaviors are required. STUDENT:	Individual Target Behavior	Comes on Time to Class & Is Prepared	Completes Assigned Work	Follows Teacher Directions	Appropriate Verbal Behavior	Hall Conduct (must have a pass)	Handles Materials Appropriately	On Task Behavior (at desk)	Shop	P.E.	Art	Music	Other	TOTAL POINTS EARNED FOR BEHAVIOR	+ BONUSES FOR SPECIAL BEHAVIOR +	Record of Negative Behavior (Use Code Below)	– PENALTIES (Negative Behavior)	– PURCHASES (Breaks, etc.)	NET POINTS FOR DAY – lost + earned	CRITERION BEHAVIORS (number of 2s) *

PENALTY

Leaving class without pass	10—20	Entered _____
Refusing to do class work	10—20	Charted _____
Refusing to follow directions	10—20	
Fighting	300	
Threatening a teacher/student	10—20	Fines _____
Excessively out of seat	10—20	
Verbal outburst	10—20	
Other		

Figure 2–5. *Teacher's daily behavior report.*

- Lunch cafeteria privileges
- May purchase (for points) extra snack items
- May participate in after-school activities

Time—Must pass twenty consecutive days but is allowed one day to fail
    (not reach the minimum)
Passing standard—a minimum of five 2s

Level III

- No pass needed for bathroom
- Extra recess time allowed
- First in line for lunch
- Discounts on all purchases
- May become a teacher's helper

Time—Must complete the passing standard noted below or return to
    Level II for another twenty-day count
Passing standard—a minimum of six 2s

Generalization and Maintenance

Once a student has successfully changed and is now conforming
to your expectations, the question arises as to how long the maintenance of the contractual system needs to continue. The following
points should be considered when answering this question:

1. Behavior changed in one class may not necessarily be changed in
   others or at home. Rewards and contracts tend to be very
   localized as to their relative effects.
2. Withdrawal of the reward system can likely bring about a gradual
   return of the disruptive behavior.
3. The reward system can be reduced or the rewards shifted
   gradually from tokens or materials to social rewards with little
   danger of having a relapse of the disruptive behavior.
4. Teacher feedback to the student on a daily basis as to how the
   contract is holding up is mandatory.

Time-Out Rooms

The use of a room or area in the classroom where a disruptive student can be sent has proved to be an essential management technique. It is punishing enough for a student to be asked to withdraw from social interaction. However, the real value of a time-out area for the students is that it allows them to calm down, focus, and to clarify the issues that caused removal from the class. Once a student has had a chance to recover his/her composure, you can apply one or more of the other discipline techniques discussed.

Some points to remember:

1. Describe to the class early in the year the location and purpose of the time-out area, and those disruptive behaviors that will result in a student being asked to go to the area.

2. Emphasize repeatedly during the school year that being sent to the time-out area is *not* punishment, but an opportunity for a student to be by him/herself and to calm down.

3. Never use a time-out area to excess. It should not be a substitute for attempting any of the other confrontation procedures.

4. Only send students to the time-out area for short periods of time.

5. When sending students to the area, make sure you have given them work to do while there.

Figure 2–6 summarizes the behavior modification program.

Procedure

    1. Label behavior in concrete terms.
    2. Observe behavior.
    3. Negotiate reasons for change and consequences for not changing.
    4. Establish a contract.
    5. Determine a renewal date.

Four Sample Behavior Modification Programs
Generalization and Maintenance
Time-Out Rooms

Figure 2–6. *Behavior modification review.*

GROUP CONTINGENCY CONTRACTING

This behavior change technique is similar to the orientation of behavior modification discussed previously. Like behavior modification, the teacher is interested in changing primarily behavior, not thoughts or feelings. The teacher imposes a structure for change, uses rewards, and contracts with students. The chief difference with this technique is that it incorporates the dynamics of peer pressure and peer support to help produce change. These peer dynamics, as anyone who works with students knows, are very powerful influencers of behavior. With this technique, the teacher utilizes these natural social forces to implement behavior change.

When to Use

This technique is appropriate to use both with individuals and with the entire class. If a teacher has difficulty finding rewards to implement a behavior modification program for an individual student, it may be necessary to use the natural social rewards that exist in the classroom among students. A student may show little enthusiasm for gaining behavior points to attend a field trip, but if his/her behavior was one of the factors influencing the amount of break time for the entire class, the social pressure to conform would be hard to resist. In addition, there are times when the behavior of most students in the room is considered inappropriate. Rather than laboriously establishing behavior modification programs for each student, a group contract would be more efficient and probably more effective.

Types of Group Contracting

There are three types of group contingency contracting. Examples have been provided here to illustrate each type. The third type of contracting is perhaps the most useful employment of group pressure and, therefore, the most powerful.

1. *Single.* In this type of group contracting, one individual must change his behavior if the whole class is to receive the reward. This type is effective with hyperactive students and those who regularly come to class late or without their homework. For example, if Paul is getting out of his seat every five minutes to talk to other students, sharpen pencils, or just to move about the room, the teacher might state that if Paul can keep

his movements down to only two out-of-seat behaviors, then the entire class will get three minutes added on to their break time. The only time this type of group contracting is not recommended is when the behavior of the individual targeted for change is based on biological or physical causes. Remember, group contracting works because of social factors and has almost no effectiveness if the student cannot control behavior physiologically.

2. *Individualization.* Here each student must perform differently if he/she is to receive a reward. The same targets or criteria are used for each student. In this instance, individual contracts are actually established, but the contracts are the same for everyone and whether a student completes the contract or not is public knowledge. For example, the teacher announces that each student who completes all the written work for the day and receives a grade of eighty percent or better on the work will be given an announced reward. In another example, the teacher puts each student's name on the board and every time the student talks out of turn or gets out of his/her seat, a mark is put under the name. At the end of the day or class period, all those students who had two or less marks will get no homework or extra recess time.

3. *All.* In this case, the whole class must conform to a single criterion if the rewards are to be applied to the entire class. If the class, as a whole, fails to reach the target or desired level of change, then no one is rewarded. The teacher can set criteria, such as that ninety percent of the class must complete the daily assignment, or that ninety-eight percent of the class must be in the room when the class bell rings. Or the teacher may want to calculate averages that the class must maintain in its academic work if it is to receive a reward. This type of contracting is effective with behavior excesses such as talkativeness, aggression, and out-of-seat behavior. Two examples are presented here which are effective in changing student behavior.

Example One: A teacher can reduce the rate of talking-out behavior of an entire class by stating that they would be allowed to leave five minutes early, receive no homework, or be allowed a five-minute break if they accumulated less than fifteen marks on the board. Each mark would represent an instance of a student talking out, and the teacher would record the mark immediately after the behavior occurred for the entire class to see. What usually happens with this technique is that the class accumulates ten marks very quickly, but abruptly reduces its rate as the total approaches the "fifteen mark." Peer control and the desirability of the reward help this technique work. Over a period of time, the teacher can reduce the total number of marks from fifteen to ten to eight to five, until talking-out behavior is eliminated. The rewards can also be gradually eliminated.

Example Two: A teacher can reduce the rate of absences or class lateness by placing a very large graph on the wall, listing the days of the week on the horizontal axis and the number of incidences of class absence or lateness on the vertical axis. Chart the rate for the class from day to day, and then set a level at which you will reward the class with a party. This level may be ninety-eight percent attendance or one hundred percent on-time performance. Keep the graph up-to-date to show the class how it is performing. Ask the class for further suggestions on how to keep the performance at the accepted level.

Procedure

Once the teacher has chosen the behavior to be changed, the behavior should be charted prior to implementation of contracting. Determine, for example, what amount of out-of-seat behavior exists before attempting to change it. Once this rate has been charted, choose a level of the behavior that would be acceptable. Never expect one hundred percent of the students to maintain the acceptable level of behavior one hundred percent of the time; if you do, your group contingency plan will collapse.

For your first week of implementation, set a behavior level somewhat below the level you have chosen as unacceptable. As the class attains the level the first week, increase the level that will be accepted for the second week.

For example, after a week of charting, you have determined that the total number of times students get out of their seats each day ranges from fifteen to twenty. You determine that you can accept five out-of-seat movements. The first week of implementation, you might choose ten out-of-seat movements daily as acceptable. The second week make the rate eight, and the third week reduce it to your minimal accepted level of five. If the class is very cooperative, you might start the first week at ten and drop to five by the second week.

Counting the behavior(s) selected for reduction should be done via a very observable method. Use marks on the board or marbles in a jar to demonstrate to the class that you have observed the occurrence of a targeted behavior and have counted it. It is best not to even mention the fact that you are counting, as the nonverbal behavior will deliver the message and instructional rhythm and time will not be lost.

Rewarding students for achieving the behavior should be imme-diate—daily if possible. Examples of such rewards are an early release time, extra break time, extra dessert at lunch, token economy points, or a party. Keep the rewards positive; negative consequences such as missing a trip or being deprived of some item are not as effective in changing behavior.

Failure of group contingency contracting is usually for one or more of the following reasons:

1. The students' perception of the plan is that it is "unfair."
2. The targeted level of acceptable behavior is beyond that which the students can obtain.
3. Lack of consistency in implementation; you cannot enforce the plan every other day.
4. The reward is not attractive enough to the students.
5. One student consistently hampers the others from reaching the target level. (One suggestion in this instance would be to place this student under a behavior modification schedule or use a family intervention technique.)

Figure 2–7 summarizes group contigency contracting.

Types of Group Contingency Contracting

1. *Single:* One student must change if the whole class is to benefit.
2. *Individualization:* Each student who changes receives the benefit. Public knowledge of successes and failures.
3. *All:* Whole class must conform if the benefits are to be received by everybody.

Figure 2–7. *Group contingency contracting review.*

FAMILY INTERVENTION

This technique is a method of changing a student's behavior by altering the relationship between members of the family. The focus is on the whole family, not the student identified as having the problem. This method views the identified problem of the student as a symptom of communication dysfunction among family members. The problem's solution rests with the family; it is their responsibility to work it out. It is the teacher's duty to bring together the family members and help them communicate about this solution. The student manifesting problems is viewed not as a delinquent, but as a family member who has absorbed the anxiety and tension existing in the family to such a degree that it becomes visible in the student's acting out behavior.

When to Use

If a teacher cannot change the behavior of a disruptive student using one of the five techniques described earlier, two things are evident:

1. The student is using enormous energy and resistance to thwart the teacher's attempts to change the behavior.
2. The cause of this acting out behavior may well be outside the student's power to control.

A teacher at this point should consider utilizing the student's family members to help bring about change.

This technique is very useful when a school district has acting out problems with a number of children from the same family. It is very economical in that every family member is involved at once in the treatment and only a few members of a school need to be involved. Other advantages are noted in that the positive change in the student is more permanent and that the parents of disruptive students become supporting members of the school system, rather than being angry and resistant toward the system.

Procedure

Since this discipline technique may be new to you, a number of basic operating principles have been outlined to help in the orientation. At first glance, you may say that this technique makes you a family therapist. Rest assured that you are not doing therapy. What you are doing, and what numerous other teachers who have used this technique have done, is to change student behavior in the classroom. If you keep this goal in focus, you will have little difficulty obtaining a working level knowledge.

1. *Start with the presenting problem, but look for family communication problems.* The problem could be smoking pot, truancy, or general

academic failure. As the family talks about the problem, look for patterns in the manner in which individual members talk to each other about the issue: who talks to whom and when, who is the scapegoat—the one member who is blamed for all the trouble.

2. *The problem is communication, not psychodynamics.* Stay away from analyzing why someone did something. The event is in the past; it is over. You risk mind-reading or trying to figure someone out, and this information, even if it is accurate, is useless for behavior change. Remember, the problem is not truancy—or whatever it may be—but the way family members communicate with each other.

3. *State your goal.* The family members should be given a clear statement as to why they are at the meeting. For example, one purpose could be, "Let's get Katie to do her homework." Discuss with them your concerns and ask for help to develop a plan to ensure that Katie gets her work done.

4. *Set rules for communication.* A few rules are necessary in any family meeting. Some examples:

- No one is to interrupt another.
- No one is to speak for another.
- Everyone should look at the person they are addressing.
- No physical violence.

You will find that all but the last rule, physical violence, will be violated in most meetings. When they are violated, comment on the fact. The typical response from the violator will be anger or embarrassment, but the other family members will receive some insight into how the family miscommunicates.

5. *Ask each family member how they view the problem.* This procedure will allow each individual the opportunity to say something and also to be heard by the others. You will be surprised at how they can have differing views. Try to start the individuals to comment on what each said.

6. *Determine family roles.* Under stress most families revert to predetermined role-playing (Satir 1972). Some individuals become blamers by accusing other members of causing the problem. Some become placaters by trying to preserve family harmony, avoid conflicts, and do things for others. Some become computers by reacting with little or no emotion and seeming calm. They often say intelligent things but never become involved. Some become distracters when they start talking off the subject, answer a question with a question, or try to make the conversation frivolous.

7. *Reframe events for the family.* A tactic for changing a family's reaction to an event or problem is to change its view of the situation. Place the problem in a new emotional or conceptual setting which fits the facts. For example, a girl who stays home from school could be described not as a truant, but as an individual who loves her mother very much. Or another example, comment on the fact that each family member must really care about each other to come to a meeting like the one you are holding.

8. *Recognize anger as hurt.* If someone becomes angry it means they are hurt. State this to the family when it happens and notice how individuals will react differently to the individual being angry.

9. *Avoid advice-giving.* If you give advice you will be seen by one or more family members as taking sides. You will no longer be a neutral influence and will not be able to get family members communicating. If asked, just say, "I need more information before I can say something."

10. *Don't force people to talk.* Some family members, particularly the one with the identified problem, may not say anything. It is best to just let this person hear the conversation about the facts. If you pursue this person, he/she will distance themselves more. If you leave him/her alone, he/she may pursue you and others and become involved.

11. *Avoid the family "we."* Family members often cannot differentiate themselves from each other. For example, "It is always the parents against the kids." This statement negates anything any individual may think or feel about an issue. Ask family members to take "I" positions so they are clearly heard about an issue. No one will have an excuse to mind-read or put thoughts in another's head.

12. *Families have neither victims nor victimizers.* If you start to feel that one individual member is really receiving all the negative feelings and actions from others, or if you feel one individual is the cause of all the difficulties in the family, you have moved yourself emotionally into the family's dynamics. Keep an objective mind-set. Remember, it takes two to communicate in a family. One cannot be a "good" family member without a "bad" member helping them to look good.

13. *Membership.* Family members should be thought to include not only those living under the same roof as the student, but also others who have influence over the student. In divorced families, certainly both parents should be present, as well as any new step-fathers or step-mothers. Grandparents may be helpful, as well as uncles and aunts who have a say in the family.

14. *Recognize your limitations.* You will see a lot of miscommunication, mistrust, lack of intimacy, and hurt in these family meetings. You will not

be able to change much of this, but you will be able to make some impact on how members relate at least to one individual for at least a short time. You may affect all family members somewhat, but families are very resistant to change. Remember, your goal is the specific behavior change in that one student.

INTERVENTION EXAMPLE:
THE FAMILY MEETING

This strategy focuses on a meeting with the student, the parents, and other family members. The reason for the meeting called by you is to discuss your problem of changing the behavior of the student in your class. The problem should be defined in a concise, clear statement. The meeting should not last longer than one and one-half hours and every family member should be asked to attend. The message you are sending is that it is a family problem now, as well as a school problem.

For the meeting bring as much data as you have available to support your charges that the problem is indeed a problem. Most parents do not have access to the files or reports you may have. You want to reveal all the facts which are not known and review those you may have already mentioned. Everyone at the meeting then starts at the same point with the same facts. Typical school data you may find useful: copies of student's attendance record, report card, permanent record card, relevant teacher comments, any discipline referrals, or you class grade book.

Part I

Thank everyone for coming to the meeting and recognize any hardships this may have caused. State the goal of the meeting and emphasize the severity of the problem. During this part you should do most of the talking. After all, the meeting is for your agenda, and you want to establish yourself as being in control, confident, direct, and structured.

Talk about the problem in non-emotional terms. Avoid confronting the student directly. The emphasis should be on the facts or data you brought with you. As you present these facts, the focus of everyone's attention should be on the data, not the student with the problem. The facts will speak for themselves as to the severity of the problem.

During this part of the meeting your goal is to have everyone view the problem as clearly as possible. Often myths or magical thinking evolve, indicating that everything will be okay or that if we just have a pep talk things will improve. To accomplish your goal swamp them with data.

Part II

At this point in the meeting your goal is to get family members to talk to each other about the problem. You will do less and less talking and more and more facilitating of the conversation. The best technique to use to start the conversation is to ask each member how he/she views the facts just reviewed. Many values, judgments, opinions, and disagreements will be expressed. Point out similarities and differences of opinion. Ask members to talk to each other, not to you.

The discussion will often become intense, and the family members will try to "dump" everything on some member—usually the identified problem student. Remember to use the procedures discussed earlier—rule setting, reframing, recognizing hurt, "I" positions, and commenting on who talks to whom—to keep the family members talking about how they talk or do not talk to each other.

It is not important that family members actually recognize the problem as one of family communication, because by discussing the issue with one another they are dealing with it as a family concern. When you feel the discussion has explored the problem somewhat, or some insight has been gained about the family's communication patterns, or when you feel each member has had or is capable of having some meaningful talk with each other member, it is time to move the family into Part III.

Part III

The goal of this part of the meeting is to set up strategies for change in the student's behavior. You will need the family members' help to solve the problem. Ask the family if they tried anything in the past to address the issue. Ask if any of the parents have a similar problem and/or a solution for it which could offer some insight. It is important to remind family members of previous difficulties with this issue so that they realize how problematic it can be. They will then also be more open to suggestions from you.

A number of common strategies have been used with success. These can either be used together or taken one at a time.

1. Set up a behavior modification program where regular privileges at home now become contingent on a change of behavior at school. Use of the TV, stereo, video machine, treats, allowance, presents, car rides, and going out privileges are now to be earned. The teacher will call each day to report on whether a behavior change has occurred. If it has, the parents will reward the student with the agreed-upon privilege. This privilege and only this privilege will be covered by the behavior to be questioned. Make it clear to the parents that they should not make other conditions like taking out the garbage prerequisites to gaining the privilege.

2. Ask the parent who has least time to spend with the student to spend more time with him or her. Have this parent become your link to the home. You want the student to start building deeper ties with all members of his/her family. You accomplish this by having them talk to each other.

3. Ask the student to accomplish a specific task, such as visiting grandparents and asking what it was like when his/her parent was in school and what kind of problems and solutions existed. Your goal here is to help the student view the family beyond the immediate household. Help the student realize that he/she is not alone with a problem that ever existed before. When divorce and remarriage are factors, have the student interview and discuss with you the answers of all parties of the extended family.

4. Ask the family to pick a time and place to meet on a regular basis to deal with ongoing problems. These meetings should be open to all family members to mention anything they want. Topics which relate to everyone's needs, such as living arrangements, money, food, duties, and vacations could be proposed.

Part IV

This part of the meeting concerns outcome. One question you may ask is what the student's reaction to all this family intervention will be. Generally, students are at first angry and resentful that you have brought in their family. Students who have reached the point where nothing else works to change their behavior don't want to change. Bringing in their family is sensed as breaking the rules. They believe what happens at home remains at home, and what happens in school should remain in school. However, the student will begin to feel a sense of respect and perhaps awe that you can bring the family together to talk about his/her behavior. Once the family dynamics begin to operate, the student will lose sight of you and become enmeshed in the family communication processes. During the behavior modification program the student will react to you in one of two ways. The student may continue to ignore you and avoid verbal interaction. This behavior, coupled with behavior change in school, will suggest that family dynamics are a very powerful force in changing this student. If the student starts to verbally interact with you, even slightly, and there is evidence of behavioral change, you can be sure the student is looking at you as a buffer from the power of the family dynamics.

If by chance the student still refuses to change behavior, he/she is now not only resisting you and the school, but also resisting the family. The issue is now a family problem. Community resources are often needed at this point to serve the needs of this student.

Figure 2–8 summarizes the family intervention program.

The family is the focus of the intervention, not the individual student.

1. Look for communication problems.
2. Take control of the meeting.
3. Make comments on how the family communicates.
   - Reframing
   - "I" statement
   - Anger is hurt
   - Individual perspectives on the problem
   - Family roles

Intervention: Family Meeting

Part I: Data confrontation
Part II: Family discussion of data
Part III: Determining a strategy for change
Part IV: Outcomes

Figure 2–8. *Family intervention review.*

NINE STEPS TOWARD IMPLEMENTATION

There are nine steps to consider if you want to successfully implement one of the discipline techniques discussed in this chapter:

Step 1: Consider your needs. What do you want to happen? What do you want changed?

Step 2: Consider the student's needs. Refer back to Figure 2–1 (on page 48), which outlines techniques and needs.

Step 3: Pick a discipline technique appropriate to both needs.

Step 4: Pick a backup technique in case you get stuck.

Step 5: Decide what you will do if both plans fail.

Step 6: Implement discipline technique.

Step 7: Stop, focus on the process. Ask yourself if it is going where you want to go.

Step 8: Continue to implement the technique or move to backup if necessary.

Step 9: Assess what happened at the conclusion of the technique. What would you do differently next time?

The following dialogue between a teacher and student is from an actual transcript. It shows how the teacher used two different discipline techniques discussed in this chapter to produce some behavioral change.

Example

Mrs. Smith, an English teacher, decides that Michael's chronic lateness to class must end. She decides that it is necessary to confront Michael, but as he is late for class eighty-five percent of the time, it would be best accomplished at the end of the day during eighth period, when no other students are around to influence him.

Mrs. Smith anticipates that Michael's response will be that of a verbally aggressive student, but that he is capable of developing a plan to change. In light of this, she opts to utilize a reality therapy procedure. However, if Michael's aggression becomes too intense, she will plan to implement assertive techniques and move into a behavior modification procedure if he is unwilling to change.

MRS. SMITH: Michael, I want to talk to you about your pattern of coming to class late on most days. What are you doing? (Reality Therapy Procedure)

MICHAEL: Aw, Mrs. Smith, you know
              I have to hustle to get to
              your room. Besides, you
              never teach anything in-
              teresting, so why should
              I?

MRS. SMITH: Your lateness bothers me.
              What and how I teach are
              not the issues right now.
              How is coming late help-
              ing you?   (Reality Therapy
                                                    Procedure)

MICHAEL: The issue is you're a lousy
              teacher...[laugh]

MRS. SMITH: [Silent—just stares at
              Michael.]

MICHAEL: Well...look at you stand-
              ing like that...[laugh]...
              What do you want, Mrs.
              Smith? You want me to
              come early?

MRS. SMITH: How would that help
              you?   (Reality Therapy
                                                    Procedure)

MICHAEL: You tell me.

MRS. SMITH: What I want, Michael, is
              for you to be in your seat
              when the bell rings. Do
              you want to try that? Can
              you do that?   (Reality Therapy
                                                    Procedure)

MICHAEL: Can you make your class
              interesting? Can you do
              that? [Mimics her tonal
              inflection.]

At this point Mrs. Smith realizes that Michael is not responding
to her attempts to change his behavior. She therefore decides that she
must assert her rights and use some assertive responses.

MRS. SMITH: Michael, I want you in
              class tomorrow on time.

MICHAEL:	And if I'm not...	
MRS. SMITH:	I want you in class on time tomorrow.	(Persistence Technique)
MICHAEL:	How about your teaching?	
MRS. SMITH:	You may be right; perhaps my teaching could use some tightening up ...but I want you in class on time tomorrow.	(Persistence Technique)
MICHAEL:	We'll see...	
MRS. SMITH:	Yes I will, because I want you in class on time tomorrow.	(Persistence Technique)
MICHAEL:	And if I don't?	
MRS. SMITH:	Frankly, Michael, if you do not show up for class on time, the following things will happen: • I will place you in the time-out corner of the room for the entire class period. You can work there. • This will continue each day you are late. • There will be no discussion of this, you will just do it. Now, Michael, are there any questions about what will happen?	(Behavior Modification Technique)
MICHAEL:	No, I'll see you tomorrow.	

Michael leaves having modified his original defiant attitude that he would not come to class on time. The verbal aggression has disappeared. The teacher's approach was well planned and her message delivered in a clear, concise, demanding manner. Did Michael change his behavior? He did come to class the next day—on time.

REFERENCES

Alberti, Robert E. *Assertiveness*. San Luis Obispo, California: Impact Publishers, 1977.

Brammar, Lawrence M. *The Helping Relationship, Process and Skills*. Englewood Cliffs, New Jersey: Prentice-Hall, 1973.

Carkhuff, R. R.; D. Kratochril; and T. Friel. "Effects of Professional Training: Communication and Discrimination of Facilitative Conditions," *Journal of Counseling Psychology, 15,* 1968, 68–74.

Curwin, Richard, and Allen Mendler. *The Discipline Book: A Complete Guide to School and Classroom Management*. Englewood Cliffs, New Jersey: Prentice-Hall, 1980.

DeRisi, William J., and George Butz. *Writing Behavioral Contracts*. Champaign, Illinois: Research Press, 1975.

Dyer, Wayne W. *Your Erroneous Zones*. New York: Funk & Wagnalls, 1976.

Glasser, William E. *Reality Therapy*. New York: Harper & Row, 1965.

Gordon, Thomas. *Teacher Effectiveness Training*. New York: McKavy, 1974.

Jones, Norman. *Keep in Touch: How to Communicate Better by Responding to the Feeling Instead of the Event*. Englewood Cliffs, New Jersey: Prentice-Hall, 1981.

Satir, Virginia. *Peoplemaking*. Palo Alto, California: Science and Behavior Books, 1972.

Smith, Manuel J. *When I Say No, I Feel Guilty*. New York: Dial Press, 1975.

Stierlin, Helm; Ingeborg Rucker-Embden; Norbert Wetzel; and Michael Wirsching. *The First Interview with the Family*. New York: Brunner/Mazel, 1980.

Sulzer, Beth, and G. Roy Mayer. *Behavior Modification Procedures for School Personnel*. Hinsdale, Illinois: Dryden Press, 1972.

Wolfgang, Charles H., and Carl D. Glickman. *Solving Discipline Problems: Strategies for the Classroom Teacher*. Boston: Allyn and Bacon, 1980.

Confrontation Strategies

Confrontation is defined operationally as the process whereby a teacher attempts to stop an angry, disruptive student from acting out. It is not necessarily the process of trying to change a student's behavior to something more positive (although this may be desired), but rather the process of changing very negative behavior to that of a more neutral position. Once this is accomplished, the teacher may want to move toward a positive change by implementing one of the six discipline procedures discussed in Chapter 2.

The teacher who fails to realize that an angry or disruptive student must first be brought to a position of neutrality before change procedures can be implemented, will often meet with frustration, anger, and possibly even physical harm. An example of this can be seen in the situation in which a student is about to throw a chair across the aisle at another student because of a remark made. An inappropriate remark for the teacher to make would be:

"Billy, put the chair down and get back to work."

In this case, the teacher is telling Billy to move from feeling very angry to becoming positively motivated to work. There is an absence of a middle or neutral step which is critical if Billy is going to defuse himself and put the chair down. In addition, one cannot demand that someone stop being angry, assaultive, or disruptive. This procedure rarely works and, when it does not, only serves to negate your credibility. You cannot, however, ignore such extremely negative behavior. The procedures described in this chapter will provide ways to stop angry, disruptive students.

SEVEN OPERATIONAL GUIDELINES

The following procedures are important to remember during a confrontation.

1. Keep a Low Threshold for Disruption

Keep your classes so well structured that any behavior that is negative, disruptive, or potentially harmful is clearly evident. When disruption occurs, stop instruction and deal with the behavior as if it were the most critical issue of the day. There are numerous techniques described in Chapter 1 which will enable you to manage and structure a class so as to avoid disruptions.

2. Negotiate

View all confrontation as negotiation. Calculate how much a student is willing to move from a very negative position to one of neutrality and how much one has to contribute to make this happen. Stick to your goal in the confrontation and try to ignore abuse or insults from the student. Avoid dumping your own emotional concerns on the student and do not humiliate the student. Give the student the feeling that he/she must change, but the manner of that change can be discussed. It is possible to seek options and alternatives from the student first, before calling up your own plan. A remark such as "How can we solve this disagreement?" gives the student some face-saving options but clearly keeps you in control of the situation. In our example of the boy about to throw the chair, you could say:

"Billy, put the chair down so we can decide how to solve this disagreement."

In another more subtle example, a teacher asked a boy to put his shirt on in class. The student asked why, announced to the class that the female teacher was in love with his body, and tried to ignore the teacher. The teacher asked again, using a verbal technique discussed later in this chapter. At this point the student realized he was going to have to change. However, he asked to go to the bathroom. The teacher gave permission, knowing the student had changed the subject and had not put on his shirt. When the student returned a few minutes later, the shirt was on and the student sat down without saying a word. The teacher won the confrontation, and the student won by not losing face in front of his friends.

3. Deal with That Observed

Confront only the behavior that happens in the present. For example

"Carol, you are five problems behind the rest of the class."

Avoid mentioning the student's past record by saying something like

"You are five problems behind and you have been each day this week. You now are twenty problems behind the class."

Students often forget transgressions committed yesterday or in the past. They often will argue with your memory of the event. You can win your confrontation and get the student on task by dealing with the present transgression, so avoid possible arguments over the past.

Avoid probing the student's mind by asking questions as to why the behavior is occurring. Students often do not know why they transgress; and even if they do know, they are not about to tell you.

Avoid trying to interpret a student's disruptive behavior by guessing a motive. This is called mind reading. For example

"The reason you are five problems behind every day is that you are trying to irritate me."

4. Express a Clear Goal

Before you confront verbally or nonverbally, know your goal. What do you want the student to change? Express this goal in a direct, even blunt manner. Do not apologize for the rules; do not seek the student's·approval for the confrontation. Using the example cited earlier:

"Billy, put the chair down now. The rule says no chair throwing. I say no chair throwing."

5. Use Direct Language

When you make your confrontation to the student and express your goal, use personal pronouns, express personal feelings, and ask direct questions. Your confrontation will sound stronger and be more successful. Examples are

"I want you to do better."

rather than

"I want your English grades to be better."
"Paul, you are asleep again."

rather than

"Some of you are always asleep."
"How does swearing at me help you?"

rather than

"Why are you swearing at me?"

If a student disagrees with your instructions or claims he/she is doing what you said, disagree with a student's opinion or interpretation of the rules and emphasize your own feelings and thoughts:

"No, that is not what I said, and I want you to listen to me more carefully next time."

6. Have a Bottom Line

Know what resources you can call on if your confrontation fails to change student behavior. This could be calling on a supervisor, a parent, or even the police. Your bottom line should be a source which is immediately available, can move the student out of the classroom, and will support your goal. You rarely have to express or threaten the bottom line as an option to students. They usually know in each particular building what it is; and if you need to use it once, they will remember it.

Don't use your bottom line in every situation. Continuous use or even threatening to use it makes you look weak in front of the class. On the other hand, if a student continues to defy you because he/she does not want to lose face in front of peers or for whatever reason, you will need to explain the bottom line to the student as a natural consequence of this defiance. One way it could be done:

"Okay, Billy, you refuse to put the chair down and discuss this disagreement with Mike. I will need to call Mr. Owens from across the hall to remove you from the classroom. Do you want to go through all that hassle over such a disagreement?"

7. Follow-Up

Once the confrontation has passed and some behavior change has occurred, you should make a point of speaking to the student later in the day. Often a simple remark is all that is needed to maintain a good relationship with the student. Remember, you will probably have this student all year. Follow-up establishes closure on the event and keeps the student on positive terms with you. The student may need to be confronted again in the future, and starting off from a base of mutual respect and understanding would be helpful. For example

"Sorry things reached such dramatic proportions this morning."
"Thanks for the talk earlier."
"I felt good about what you did."
"How has the rest of the day been?"

THREE NONVERBAL TECHNIQUES

Yes, you can confront nonverbally as well as verbally. Students perceive your nonverbal confrontation, usually unconsciously, before they do your verbal confrontation. In fact, you can confront a student nonverbally, but you cannot confront a student just verbally. Nonverbal behavior involves how you move your arms, legs, body, head, and eyes to communicate a message. The three techniques described here, when used to support a verbal confrontation, can make your statement very powerful and, therefore, more effective.

1. Body Congruence

Research has shown that matching the arm and leg positions of another when speaking will result in the other person perceiving you as more empathetic and understanding. A method some confronters use to communicate to the student that they want to understand his/her point of view is to match the arm and leg positions of the student. This is simply a matter of positioning your arms and legs in a mirror image of the position held by the student. If the student sitting in front of you has his left leg outstretched with his right leg crossing over at the ankle, you stretch out your right leg and cross your left leg at the ankle. Or if a student has his left hand on the chair and his right one in a pocket, you face the student and put your right hand on the chair and your left hand in your pocket (if you have no pocket, rest it in the general area).

If the student gestures or scratches during the confrontation you should maintain the original body position, because in most cases the student will return to the position he/she was in initially. After a few minutes, or when you feel the student is starting to hear you and negotiate, move your arms and legs out of congruence. Usually the student will shift his/her position as well (although not necessarily in the same manner), indicating that you have some control over the student's nonverbal behavior. This method is excellent to use with students who, in approaching you, have a somewhat defiant stance— with tightly folded arms or with hands on hips—and are so involved with their own concerns and with what is being said that they do not realize what you are doing. If you can change their nonverbal behavior, a change in their verbal behavior is not far behind.

2. Personal Space

Since in any confrontation you are trying to get a student to change disruptive behavior, it is appropriate to make the student feel uncomfortable enough so that change can be initiated. In Western culture it is not socially appropriate for individuals to engage in a conversation standing closer than three to four feet apart. Being within three feet of another implies intimate conversation. When you confront a student, step closer than the culturally accepted three-foot personal distance. If you are sitting at a school desk or in a chair, move your desk or chair to touch that of the student. What generally will happen is that the student will become disrupted and confused and feel uncomfortable. He or she will attempt to move away to maintain the three-foot distance. When this happens, move in closer again to maintain the nonverbal confrontation.

Another method to force a student to change is to move closer than the accepted three feet, but position yourself somewhat to the left or right of the student. In this case, the student generally will turn his/ her body in an attempt to face you. Our culture again dictates that two individuals should maintain direct body orientation when communicating. Once you have made the student turn, you have communicated to the student that you can change at least part of his/her behavior.

3. Body Positions

The following five nonverbal behaviors should be adopted when confronting a student. They give your message a clear, strong, honest directive.

Body swivel. Hold your body still when confronting the student and avoid moving or shifting your weight from foot to foot.

Eye gaze. Look directly at the face of the student. Ask the student to look at you if he/she is looking down or avoiding you. If the student cannot look at you, then position yourself so as to meet his/her eyes. If the student is looking at the floor, bend down as if you are trying to establish eye contact. The exaggerated pose will show the student how absurd his/her head position is.

Object fidgeting. Avoid holding objects when you confront a student. Put pens, books, or purse down and leave your body free of obstruction. Avoid fidgeting with jewelry, hair, glasses, or clothes.

Head nodding. Avoid head movements as they can give the impression you are agreeing with things the student is saying. Keep your head position centered.

Speaking rate. State your position and command frequently and elaborate on it. You should be doing the talking, not the student, at least not until he/she has calmed down.

FOUR VERBAL TECHNIQUES

Many students, when they are angry and disruptive, have a limited perception of what happened. Because of this they see few choices open to them and therefore believe they have no alternative but to continue to be angry and disruptive. Confronting a student's perception of what happened can be the key to opening up for that individual the complexity of reality and the wide range of options available in responding to events. In other words, behavior change occurs when perceptual change is initiated.

Listed below are four of the most common limitations students impose on their view of the events. Methods of confronting each are described. (The following material is reprinted by permission of the author and publisher. Richard Bandler and John Grinder. *The Structure of Magic I*, Palo Alto, California: Science and Behavior Books, 1975.)

1. Confront Deletions

Individuals often select and represent only parts of events and choose to delete other parts. These deletions may or may not constitute a useful tactic for an individual. A teacher may want to help the student recover these deleted portions to determine whether they were discarded by choice or were absent totally from the perception of reality.

> STUDENT: I can't learn that stuff.
>
> Here the teacher needs to challenge the noun "stuff" to allow the student to be specific about which part of the material he can't learn. Is it all the material? Probably not. What is being deleted here?
>
> TEACHER: What stuff can't you learn?
>
> As teachers, we know that others have learned the material. Therefore, our model of reality includes learning. The student's model has deleted learning the material as an option. A teacher should challenge the different model.
>
> TEACHER: What is it that stops you from learning the material?

2. Confront Distortions

Another manner in which individuals become constricted is by turning an ongoing process into an event. They perceive an action as completed and therefore their choice of response is limited. This type of distortion is called *nominalization*. A teacher may want to help the student see that what is perceived as a finished act may actually be influenced by other behaviors.

> STUDENT: Your attitude makes me mad.

There are two nominalizations here, "attitude" and "mad." The student has taken two processes and made them into completed actions, as revealed in his choice of using nouns ("attitude" and "mad") and not verbs. The teacher needs to challenge these nominalizations and allow the student the opportunity to view the event as still occurring (and therefore open to change) or closed (as it is presently viewed).

TEACHER: What is it that I do to you (challenging "attitude") that prevents you from getting along with me (challenging "mad")?

or

What would happen if you saw me differently?

3. Confront Generalizations

A third type of limitation is one in which a student chooses to take one experience or occurrence and use it as a model for all similar experiences. A teacher would want to insure that the student is able to enjoy the richness and detail present in each new experience.

STUDENT: Nobody in this school likes me.

The word "nobody" is a generalization as it has no reference point and thus relates to nothing specific. A teacher would want to determine the limits of "nobody."

TEACHER: You mean nobody in this school ever liked you?

Other examples are:

STUDENT: It's boring to sit in this class.

TEACHER: Who is bored? In what way, specifically? In what part of this class?

STUDENT: People should listen to what others say.

TEACHER: Who should, specifically? Who are the others? What are they saying?

4. Confront Cop-Outs

The last limitation occurs when the student places responsibility for feelings and behavior outside him/herself. This is called a cop-out. A student perceives others as influencing his/her actions or claims to know the thoughts and emotions of another person. A teacher may want to challenge these assumptions so as to provide a student with a different perception and, thus, alternatives of action.

One type of cop-out is called *cause-effect*.

STUDENT: You make me mad.

Here the student assumes that the teacher can control his/her emotions; his/her ability to feel mad or not is totally in the teacher's control. The student sees the teacher's act as causing the emotion, rather than the emotion as a response that he himself has generated.

> TEACHER: How do I make you mad?

This response asks the student to explore more thoroughly the process of events that led to his/her feeling angry.
Another type of cop-out is *mind reading*.

> STUDENT: The principal is a grouch and he dislikes me.

In this case the student reports that he is capable of knowing what the principal is thinking. He may or may not be right; however, the process of how he arrived at such a perception must be challenged. At the core of this limitation is the possibility that a student is projecting his feelings onto the principal without enough data to back up the assumption.

> TEACHER: How, specifically, does a grouch act?

Here the teacher is asking the student to behaviorally describe his perceptions by focusing on the specifics of who, what, where, and when. Assume the student gives the following reply:

> STUDENT: A person is a grouch if he walks with his head down and doesn't say hello.
>
> TEACHER: How, specifically, does the principal's putting his head down and not saying hello to you make you feel he dislikes you?

The teacher is challenging the student's assumption that these specific acts on the part of the principal are signs that he dislikes the student. A further response would reverse the relationship.

> TEACHER: Then, if the principal were to lift his head and say hello to you, he likes you?

HOW TO HANDLE THREATS

There are times when confrontation will produce threatening remarks from the student. In most cases, the threat is an attempt by the student to manipulate the negotiation process. It is part gaming, part impulsiveness, and always an attempt to get the teacher to back down from the stated demand.

Most threats come in the "if...then" form: "If you don't get off my case, I'll tear your hair out." It is natural for a teacher to respond to the latter part of the statement—it is the threat and what the student wants you to respond to. However, a good confronter will respond not to the latter part of the threat, but to the "if" portion. This section is the weak link in the threat, and the point where the negotiation can persist. Some typical responses to the "if" section are

1. Challenge the assumption.

STUDENT: If you don't get off my case...
TEACHER: What case? How do you know I'm on it?

2. Ask for alternatives.

STUDENT: If you don't shut up...
TEACHER: Tell me how to do it gracefully

or

Can we solve this thing?

or

I will listen to your ideas now.

3. Emphasize feelings.

STUDENT: If you don't get out of here...
TEACHER: I would like to because I'm uncomfortable, but I would like to settle this.

or

I feel I must remind you of the rules.
I'm trying...

When a teacher perceives that a threat is real and that the student has stated his/her bottom line in the negotiation process, it is best that the teacher terminate the confrontation for the moment. To persist might lead to an exchange of blows, in which case the teacher will lose the negotiation with the student forever. Remember, confrontations do not have to be resolved immediately.

In some cases a parent or principal conference might be necessary for the negotiation to continue. Parents or principals can serve as excellent facilitators between a student and teacher. In every case, however, the student's threat must be relayed to the parents, if for nothing else than the legal protection of the teacher. Such information tells the parents where the relationship between the student and teacher has deteriorated. Also, it is important to remember that not all teachers can relate to every student.

HOW TO HANDLE A CLASSROOM GROUP CONFRONTATION

If two students in a large class start to disrupt the instructional process because they are at odds (verbally or physically), the following procedure is helpful to demonstrate control of the situation.

1. Ask the two students to sit back-to-back in the middle of the room. As a teacher, your task is to act as a facilitator. You announce that there are three rules: (1) one person talks at a time, (2) no fighting, and (3) a compromise must be reached.

2. Ask one of the students to describe what happened. No one else can talk. Then ask the other student to describe what occurred. Usually a debate ensues as to who was at fault.

3. Allow the debate to proceed for a period of time and then ask if the students could reach some sort of compromise to solve the problem.

4. If the students cannot negotiate, then ask the other students in the class who have been watching to provide some ideas for settlement.

5. Usually the pressure to get out of the middle of the circle and the pressure from fellow classmates to settle the disagreement will result in a compromise before too long.

The following dialogue illustrates the process of a classsroom group confrontation. John and Mike, both fifth-graders, were arguing. Their noise level was so high that the entire class was being disrupted. Despite two reminders from the teacher to calm down and pay attention, John and Mike continued to argue. It was clear to the teacher that this argument needed to be resolved if the lesson was to proceed.

The teacher could send the boys down to the office or have them sit outside the door. In this case, however, the teacher decided that it was as important for her to show the other students in the class that she was capable of handling this disruption as it was for her to calm these two students down. She needed to communicate to the entire class that she was in control and had the means to confront disruption effectively. In the future when other students had a disagreement, they might think twice about disrupting her class.

TEACHER: John and Mike, I would like you both to come to the front of the class. Bring your chairs.

(While the two boys are coming forward the teacher addresses the class.)

Now class, there seems to be some sort of argument between John and Mike. We cannot continue with our lesson until the issue is settled. I may need your help, so listen carefully. Now John and Mike, I would like you to sit back-to-back in your chairs. We are going to resolve this conflict now. I have three rules for this talk we are about to have. The first is that only one of you can talk at a time; the second, that there will be no physical contact; and third, some sort of agreement to end this argument must be reached. Class, you cannot talk during this meeting. You will have a chance later. Okay, John, tell me what this argument is all about.

(The teacher moves over so that John sees her and can talk with her at ease.)

JOHN: Aw, you know Mike is always accusing me of something or other. He thinks I went into his locker and used his lousy basketball during lunch....

MIKE: Well, you did...you're a thief!

TEACHER: Now, Mike, it is not your turn to talk yet. You will get a chance. Is there anything else you need to tell me about this, John?

JOHN: Just that I do not know what he is talking about. I never saw his basketball and if I did I would not use it anyway. It has hardly any air in it.

MIKE: He is lying...liar...liar.

JOHN: Oh shut up....

TEACHER: Remember the rule, boys, one person talks at a time.
           Now, Mike, give me your version of the event.
           (Teacher moves over to Mike)

MIKE: He took my basketball, I know it. Some friends saw him
           with it. He is lying again.

TEACHER;   Well, John and Mike and class, it seems we have a real
           difference of opinion as to what happened. John says he
           didn't take the ball and Mike claims he did. Let's see if we
           can resolve this issue. Mike, what do you need to happen
           to solve this issue?

MIKE: Let me hit him. He won't take the ball again.

TEACHER: Well, no fighting is one of the rules that we have,
           remember. But I'll check it out with John.
           (Teacher moves over so John can see her)
           John, Mike says if he hits you he won't argue with you
           anymore. What do you think? Will that solve the issue for
           you?

JOHN: What are you crazy...Mike hit me?

TEACHER: (Moves back to Mike)
           Sorry, John doesn't like that idea. Have you any others?

MIKE: No!

TEACHER: (Moves over to John)
           Let me see if John has any ideas. John, how would you go
           about resolving this issue?

JOHN: Just tell him to leave me alone. Don't sit or talk with me.

TEACHER: (Moves over to Mike)
           John has an idea. He says if you leave him alone, don't sit
           or talk with him, he will leave you alone. What do you
           think? Is that acceptable to you?

MIKE: Yeah, tell him to leave me alone and stay away from my
           basketball.

TEACHER: (Moves over to John)
           Mike likes that idea. If you leave him alone, he will leave
           you alone. Is that okay with you?

JOHN: Yeah.

TEACHER: (To the class as a group)
           Well, as you have heard, John and Mike have agreed to
           end their argument. We can now get back to the business

at hand. Thank you for listening. I did not need your help this time, but perhaps next time. Thank you, John and Mike, for agreeing to end the argument. Go back to your regular desks and let's have everyone open their books to page 66.

This procedure can be accomplished in a relatively short period of time. The pressure socially to have the two participants resolve the issue is so intense that students move quickly to find common ground. Notice here that the teacher was not interested in exploring the issue of who was right or wrong. Her goal was to get the class back on task with little or no disruption, not to accuse one or the other student of stealing or lying. By having the students speak to her directly, rather than to each other, she forced the verbal interaction to progress according to her standards. If the students had been allowed to speak to each other directly, arguments would have been the result. Even with this forced structure, the students had difficulty not talking directly to each other and arguing. By having them sit in such a manner that they could not see each other, the teacher eliminated all nonverbal communication. The participants could not respond to facial gestures, sneers, smiles, or laughs which they might interpret as hostile. They could only respond to the verbal dialogue directed by the teacher.

Often during such confrontations the students observing the two in the middle try to become involved. Some may try to support their buddy in the middle by calling out remarks; others may laugh at the two; others may try to get the teacher to end what they consider a circus farce. It is the teacher's job to remind the class from time to time that rule one says only one person can talk at a time. Most students observing this confrontation tend to enjoy seeing their classmates proceed through this process. This enjoyment is acceptable because it contributes to the social pressure for the two in the middle to reach a quick compromise.

If for some reason the students in the middle cannot reach a compromise despite all your efforts, it is appropriate to enlist the help of other students in the class who are observing. Let us assume that John and Mike could not reach a mutually acceptable compromise to illustrate how to use the class as helpers.

TEACHER: Okay class, since John and Mike cannot reach a compromise I would like to hear some suggestions from the rest of you. Would anyone care to offer a way for these two boys to resolve this issue? Remember, one person at a time.

ANNE: Throw them out of the room!
(All the students laugh.)

TEACHER: Okay, let's see if that is acceptable to John and Mike. John, what do you think? Do you agree to be thrown out of class?

JOHN: No way. She's crazy. I'm not leaving. I didn't do anything.

TEACHER: How about you, Mike, would being thrown out of class be an acceptable solution to this argument?

MIKE: If John isn't leaving, I'm not leaving.

TEACHER: (To Anne)
Sorry, your idea is not acceptable to either of them. Anybody else have a plan?

JOE: How about putting them in separate parts of the room? Don't allow them to talk to each other.

TEACHER: Let's see if that is acceptable. How about it, John, Mike, is Joseph's idea acceptable to you?

JOHN: Okay.

MIKE: I can buy that.

In this example the teacher increased the pressure to resolve the problem by having the peers provide solutions. While John and Mike might be able to ignore each other's ideas to resolve the problem, it was very difficult for them to resist the ideas of their peers. They now faced the prospect of not only seeming to reject each other's ideas but also of rejecting their peers. Anne's attempt at attention and humor was handled very well by the teacher. She dealt with it as a legitimate possible solution and passed the idea along to John and Mike. In so doing, she reversed peer pressure by having John and Mike communicate directly to Anne and the others who laughed because they felt the idea absurd. Notice that the next solution proposed by Joseph was more serious and realistic. Joseph's prestige was enhanced in front of his peers as well.

This group confrontation procedure demonstrates your authority, competence, and determination to control disruption. It informs acting-out students that every time they are disruptive they must go into the middle of the class, and serves to relay the message to the class that you can handle the disruptive students.

HOW TO HANDLE AN OUT-OF-CONTROL STUDENT

Students who have violent temper tantrums or go into such a rage that they lose all control of themselves present special problems in terms of confrontation. Bringing such students from such extremely negative behavior to a neutral position requires the application of certain techniques in a certain sequence. The chief problem most teachers have in dealing with such situations is handling their own emotional feelings during the student's outburst. Referred to as emotional triggers, the sight and sound of an out-of-control student triggers off emotions inside each of us. These emotions run the gamut from fear to anger, withdrawal, guilt, helplessness, and/or depression. We each have our own emotional response to seeing, hearing, or touching the wild and desperate raw emotions that an out-of-control student displays. Being able to recognize such emotional triggers in oneself is a mandatory first step toward confronting an out-of-control student. With experience, your emotional triggers may change, but, nonetheless, some emotional response will be elicited each and every time you are in the presence of an out-of-control student. You must be careful that your emotional reaction does not interfere with your confrontation.

Prevention:
As the Storm Gathers

Most students who "lose it" give off some sort of signal that they are about to totally disintegrate. The signal varies from individual to individual, but once you have identified the early warning signal for a particular student, you can be sure that the signal will be the same each time that particular student blows up. Some typical signals are:

- Shallow chest breathing
- Staring off into space
- A rapid expression of profanity
- Quick, sporadic movements about the room
- Dilation of pupils
- Catatonic-type body posture
- Throwing an object

There are a number of techniques you can use to prevent a student from totally disintegrating if you are quick enough. The procedures listed below, if applied effectively, may spare you the messy volatile situation of trying to deal with an out-of-control student. Verbal techniques do not work at calming a student down as well as techniques which employ some nonverbal procedures. Asking a student who is very, very angry what is bothering him/her requires a linguistic response. Many students at this stage of disintegration cannot regain sufficient control to interact with you in a rational manner.

The following techniques are proven, effective prevention techniques to apply if you see that one of your students is about to lose control. If, after you implement one of these procedures, the student still seems to be very upset and about to explode, try another technique. These techiques are not mutually exclusive, and it may take the application of a few before you see signs that the student is calming down. One suggestion: If you have had experiences with a particular student losing self-control, or suspect a student has the potential, it might be a good idea to rehearse or at least make the student aware of how some of these techniques work. Later, when the student has reached a point where self-control is about to be totally lost, it will be easier to engage the student in one or more of these processes and achieve a calming result.

Prevention Technique 1: Rating. Ask the student to rate on a scale of 1 to 10 where he/she thinks his/her self-control rests. Tell the student that "1" means he/she is perfectly calm, totally in control, and has no worries. However, "10" means the student is about to have a temper tantrum, lose all control, punch or hit someone, or run away. A rating of "5" means the student is average compared to most students when it comes to self-control. Tell the student he/she may rate self-control on any number. Once the student has reported his/her number, you now have a fairly good perspective of how upset this student has become. You have also provided a means for the student to become aware, if only temporarily, of where his/her self-control rests. You now want to engage the student in a verbal interaction and ask what it is going to take to move the level of self-control down the scale a few ratings. You need to communicate to the student that it is possible to reduce one's loss of self-control even a bit. A student needs to know there is a means to recover composure because very often he/she is as afraid of losing it as you are. The following example illustrates this process. Bob is about to throw a book.

TEACHER: Tell me, Bob, where are you on a scale of 1 to 10, with "1" meaning you are at perfect self-control and are worry-free, and "10" meaning you are about to hit Terry over there, and "5" meaning you are about average when it comes to self-control compared to others in the class.

BOB: I am about an 8½. I am so mad!

TEACHER: Okay, you say you are an 8½, or a bit above average in terms of loss of control, but that you have a way to go ·before you blow it all. Is that right?

BOB: I guess so.

TEACHER: What can we do to move this scale down a point or two? I understand you are upset and I do not expect you to return to normal like most in the class right away. But I was wondering if we could bring it down a bit. Are you willing to try?

BOB: I guess so.

TEACHER: Good, let us try to figure out ways for you to relax and calm down.

Prevention Technique 2: Mirror Imaging. With this procedure you act as a verbal mirror with the student. You tell the student what he/she looks like as their rage and anger build up. Remember, students about to lose control quickly shut off incoming stimuli and perceptions and become attentive only to their hurt or angry feelings. This self-absorption feeds on itself to a point where the internal rage boils over in an outward display of raw anger. By telling a student what they look like to an outsider, you are feeding information from the outside into the system and fighting the tendency of self-absorption. With this feedback, a student can self-correct behavior to conform to the internal image of what he/she thinks others perceive. For example, a teacher confronts two girls about to fight.

TEACHER: Helen, you are standing there with your feet wide apart, your fists clenched, and your hair over one eye. And Virginia, your mouth is twisted, your hands are crossed over your chest like you are protecting yourself from something, and you both are sweating.

HELEN: So what?

TEACHER: I thought you might want to know how others are looking at you now. You both are acting in some respects like animals do before they fight each other.

VIRGINIA: That is exactly what I am going to do to Helen.

TEACHER: Virginia, do you want to look like your mouth is twisted, your hands are crossed funny, and your sweat is dripping from your face and armpits?

VIRGINIA: No.

TEACHER: Then let's find some way to settle this peacefully. Okay with you, Helen?

HELEN: If you say so.

Prevention Technique 3: Talk Behind the Back. Many students about to lose control cannot verbalize their feelings of rage, hurt, or anger. They can only vent these raw emotions in a physical, often destructive, manner. You can help the student gain an awareness of his/her feelings and help in the process of verbalizing them if you become the mouthpiece of the student. With this technique you talk for the student, verbalizing in a way all the raw feelings boiling inside the student. You may need to guess at some of the student's inner feelings, but with so much raw emotion present, it is usually pretty easy to identify the pertinent emotions. This process is cathartic for the student and has a calming effect. For example, in this case, Lynn is very upset at Tom because he told her she smelled in front of the entire class. She is about to throw a chair at Tom.

TEACHER: (Moving behind Lynn and placing her hand on her shoulder, addressing Tom)
Tom, what you just said really upset me. It was unfair and it hurt. I am embarrassed and I am going to kill you.
(Addressing Lynn)
Is that accurate?

LYNN: (She nods in agreement)

TEACHER: (Continuing to speak for Lynn)
Furthermore, I want you to say you're sorry. You really hurt me.

TOM: Okay, okay....I'll leave you alone.

TEACHER: (To Lynn)
Okay with you?

LYNN: Okay. I'm all right now.

Prevention Technique 4: Pacing Vocally. Before a student loses all self-control, there are methods to help calm the student down which rely on matching or mismatching the voice tone of the student. Whether you match the voice tone or mismatch the tone depends on whether the student is yelling or remaining soft spoken before he/she explodes. For example, if a student is yelling, shouting, or screaming at a high voice level, you should mismatch the tone or speak to the student at an average voice tone, but as you speak lower your tone. As the student starts to respond, you will notice that his/her tone will match yours and also start to lower. If you can get the student to lower his/her voice, you have calmed the emotional outburst somewhat. A student who can hear him/herself calm down, will ultimately feel him/herself calm down.

A student who is in a volatile state may speak not with a loud voice tone, but with a soft, almost gentle tone. The student can be so consumed with rage that he/she may not be able to formulate the words appropriately. Or a student may feel he/she is losing control and clench the teeth as a means to try to control these raging feelings. The words that you hear have a soft quiet tone but are, in fact, masking volatile emotions. In this case you would match the voice tone of the student as you speak and gradually increase the level of loudness. As the student starts to respond, you will notice that his/her tone will rise to match yours. When a student hears him/herself speaking at a normal tone he/she will feel more relaxed and calm.

Prevention Technique 5: Walking. Ever hear the phrase "walk it off"? Well, asking a student to take a walk around the school building, around the track, or even around the gym perimeter is effective in reducing tension and anxiety due to bottled-up rage. Often a student cannot verbalize his/her rage until he/she experiences some physical exhaustion, which helps drain off the tension.

Once a student has completed a lap or two, ask the student to talk about what happened to start this rage. Other ways to reduce the tension physically would be to provide a punching bag in the gym, or for very small children, a large stuffed animal which could be pushed and punched around.

Prevention Technique 6: Feel Blocks. Many students who are about lose control cannot verbalize their feelings for one reason or another. Very often, the feelings are so confused they escape the student's ability to identify them. Sometimes students do identify their feelings but because they are so afraid of them or afraid of losing self-control, they deny their existence. No student can calm down completely unless he/she identifies and eventually deals with his/her feelings about the issue. For this reason, you can use Feel Blocks to help a student identify and perhaps even change his/her feelings. What is attractive about these blocks is that a student does not need to verbalize feelings in order to identify and even change them. Also, by helping students externalize their feelings with the Feel Blocks, you are allowing them to deal with these feelings in a quasi-objective manner.

Feel Blocks can be constructed from small blocks of wood at least 3″ × 5″. The following feeling words can be easily painted on using brightly colored tempera paints:

Love	Hurt
Confusion	Joy
Loneliness	Boredom
Hope	Rejection
Anger	Fear
Sadness	Hate
Clarity	Neutrality

The following example illustrates how you might use Feel Blocks to help prevent a student from losing self-control.

TEACHER: Now, Dave, I have put before you a number of large blocks that are labeled with certain feelings. These blocks are called Feel Blocks and they help us identify feelings about issues. The block with no feeling word on it is a neutral block which you can use if you are confused about what your feelings may be or if you need to change your feelings, but are a bit unsure of which direction to take. I would like you to pick a block to hold or put in your pocket which best expresses how you are feeling.

DAVE: (He picks the block labeled "Anger")

TEACHER: Fine. Now I am going to pick a block labeled "Fear". The reason I feel fear is that you are so angry now, I am afraid you could hurt someone or something.

DAVE: Well, I feel angry.

TEACHER: What will need to happen to allow you to give up your "Anger" block and pick a block which has another feeling?

DAVE: What do you mean?

TEACHER: Well, if you have to pick from these blocks which emotion you would like to be feeling in a few minutes, which block would you pick?

DAVE: I wish I could pick "Clarity."

TEACHER: Why "Clarity?"

DAVE: I need to know why Elizabeth said those mean things to me. She hurt me and embarrassed me in front of my friends. I would like her to explain why.

TEACHER: So perhaps you should have two blocks. One block which says "Anger" and another which says "Hurt."

DAVE: That's right.

TEACHER: But our real goal is to have you pick up the "Clarity" block.

DAVE: Yeah.

TEACHER: Let us talk about how to do this.

At this point, the teacher can verbally engage Dave and help him calm down by planning ways to resolve his conflict. If Dave gets confused or says he doesn't care, or is unsure, the teacher could have Dave pick the "Neutral" block. The conversation now revolves around how to put down this block and pick up a block which has a feeling word on it. Identifying feelings, moving them about, and explaining why and how in this three-dimensional manner is effective at reducing the rage in students.

Prevention Technique 7: Relaxation. Teaching students how to relax seems like an odd task for a teacher. Yet it is surprising to learn how many students do not know how to begin to relax after they have become excited. Some students rely on artificial substances to calm themselves down such as drugs, alcohol, or cigarettes. The use of a progressive relaxation method is quite effective for helping very volatile students calm down. Basically, the procedure involves your directing a student to tighten and relax muscles in the body moving progressively upwards from the feet to the ankles, to the knees, and further up the body to the forehead. Major areas of the body where there are large concentrations of muscles are systematically tightened and then relaxed.

This relaxation technique helps a student gain emotional control by helping him/her to first gain physical control. Like the walking technique described earlier, progressive relaxation involves the process of physical exhaustion, in this case exhaustion of the muscle groupings. Students who have gone through this process report a much greater body awareness, deeper chest breathing, clarity of thought, and decrease in anger.

Setting: Have the student recline on the floor or stretch comfortably at the desk. Ask the student to close his/her eyes and, if possible, turn the lights off.

Procedure: Ask the student to stretch one of his/her legs out as far as possible. Then give these commands in a soft gentle voice:

Curl your toes on the left foot toward your head and then curl the toes toward the far wall. Wiggle them a bit. Feel how loose they are. Next tighten the muscles in your lower left calf, tighten, tighten, relax. (Repeat this twice.) Now tighten your left thigh, tighten, tighten, and relax. (Repeat this twice.) Repeat this procedure with the right foot, calf, and thigh.

Next relax your buttocks. Wiggle it so it fits comfortably against the floor or chair. Concentrate on how heavy your feet and legs are, how they are part of the floor. (Wait for 30 seconds.)

The next area of the body to relax is the left arm. Stretch your arm out and extend your fingers. Extend, extend, and relax. (Repeat this twice.) Now make a fist with your left hand and tighten, tighten, and relax. (Repeat this twice.) Repeat this procedure with the right hand and arm.

Concentrate on how relaxed and comfortable your arms feel. (Wait 30 seconds.)

Now we will relax your stomach and chest area. First tighten your stomach muscles, feel how tight they are, push down on the stomach area more, tighten, tighten, and relax. (Repeat this twice.) Next take a deep breath through your nose and hold it. Feel how tight your chest area feels. Hold it, hold it, exhale through the mouth. (Repeat this twice.)

Now we will relax the neck. Twist the neck around to get all the stiffness out. Pull your chin down to your chest. Release. Feel how relaxed it is.

Now relax your face. First relax the mouth by opening it wide and twisting your lips somewhat to tighten the jaw and cheek areas. Twist your nose a bit and raise your eyebrows and feel the tension in your forehead. (Repeat the face relaxation exercise twice.)

Now I want you to feel how relaxed your body has become. Feel how relaxed your left foot, your left leg, your right leg, your buttocks, your left hand, your left arm, your right hand, your right arm are. Feel how relaxed you are and how heavy your limbs are. You are breathing deeply now and feeling relaxed. (Wait 30 seconds.) I won't talk anymore. Keep your eyes closed and feel how relaxed you are. When you are ready, open your eyes. You will feel very calm and good.

Action: As the Storm Erupts

There are times when no amount of energy or involvement with any technique is going to prevent a student from losing all self-control and turning into a raving maniac. When this happens, it is important to identify the emotional trigger this behavior is turning on inside of you. Being aware of your own feelings will help you in applying the control techiques listed below and help you avoid confusing your feelings with those of the out-of-control student. The goal for all action in controlling an out-of-control student is to help the student transform the energy invested in the volatile emotions of anger, rage, and frustration into investment in emotions such as support, involvement, and control. The following techniques can be implemented when a student is totally out-of-control.

Action Technique 1: Ignoring. Often students go into rages because they are seeking the attention, concern, and sensitivity which others around them will offer. These rages are truly out-of-control behaviors because once a student starts to disintegrate, there are few chances to gain control and maintain composure. There is no turning back. In cases where you suspect the student is primarily seeking attention by a display of raw emotion, you might consider ignoring the display and denying the student the attention. This procedure is particularly attractive if the student's behavior presents no danger to self, objects, or others. Remember, it is the attention the student is seeking which should be dealt with, not the out-of-control behavior. The following story illustrates how a teacher decided to ignore the behavior of an out-of-control student in favor of addressing the need the student had for seeking attention.

Billy was a seven-year-old student sent to the main office because he turned a can of paint over on the students' work table. Billy was told to sit on the bench and wait for the principal to return. Billy was observed by the secretary as mumbling under his breath and punching his hand with his other fist. When his teacher entered the office to see how he was doing, Billy rose from the bench and flung himself to the floor. He thrashed his arms and legs out and began to foam at the mouth. He rolled around the floor, moving back and forth in a tight circle. After a minute or so Billy calmed down and began to cry. He cried for two minutes and then continued to lie on the floor resting. The teacher decided to ignore Billy's behavior and while Billy thrashed about, she watched to see that he did not hurt himself. Significantly, Billy never came close to hitting himself on the desk or bench legs. When Billy had finally come to rest and was lying on the floor breathing deeply with his eyes closed, the teacher moved over and touched him. She then decided to deal with Billy's need for attention and ignore what she and the secretary had just witnessed. She said, "Billy, are you ready to talk about what happened in the classroom? I am here to listen." With that Billy got up off the floor and began to verbalize his feelings that students in the class hated him. The teacher now could pursue the attention-seeking behavior and the hurt feelings underlying it.

Acting Technique 2: Restraining. If you suspect that a student's out-of-control behavior presents a danger to himself, others, or objects in the school, then it is necessary to restrain the student until the out-of-control behavior subsides. You may not physically have the means to do the restraining, so it may be necessary to call in some backup help. Here you may need to use your "bottom line" discussed earlier in this chapter. Regardless of whether you are doing the restraining or others are doing it, you should be aware that an out-of-control student progresses through four distinct stages before the student gains composure. During each stage, there is clear student behavior evident, specific teacher reactions, and recommended action steps.

1. *Disintegration Stage:* The student loses all self-control and starts to swear, throw things, fall on the floor, kick, foam saliva at the mouth, thrash arms and legs, or hit objects or others. This stage is marked with a release of rage in the form of raw, uncontrolled emotion.

Teacher reactions vary, but the emotional triggers usually fired are either fear or anger. Many teachers, especially the first few times, are frightened at seeing so much aggression and loss of impulse control. They fear the unknown. The other emotion is that of anger. Teachers may reciprocate the anger unleashed by the student by swearing, yelling, or even hitting the student.

Two action steps are necessary at this stage. The first is to contain the student. You would want to do this without inflicting harm on the child, but you also must maintain enough force so that the child cannot hurt him- or herself or others. It is easiest and safest to contain a child if you can put part of the child's body against a hard surface like a wall, a floor, or a desk top. In this situation you then have a firm background which protects you and the child. Another safe way to contain an acting out child is to move behind the student, reach around, cross your hands, and grab both arms of the student at the child's wrists. Pull the child's arms back so they rest crossed firmly against his/her chest. In this position the child is protected from lashing out at others or objects in the room which could cause harm.

The second action step is to talk to the student. As in the "mirror imaging" technique discussed in the prevention techniques earlier in the chapter, describe exactly how the student looks to you. For example: "You are screaming very loud, saying "damn," kicking the wastepaper basket, and sweating all over." By providing a verbal mirror for the student view him/herself, you are allowing the student to receive some feedback. The student who is consumed with emotion now has the opportunity to self-correct this image of a raving maniac to fit that self-desired, calm internal image.

2. *Composure Stage:* Once the student has vented the raw emotion, the stage in which the student tries to compose him/herself occurs. The student may rest and the body limbs may go limp. The student may become very silent or start to cry.

Teacher reactions may be a feeling of embarrassment or the need to ask questions. Because the student has moved from a very volatile stage to one of at least attempting to regain composure, the teacher may feel a bit awkward restraining a somewhat calm child. Many teachers feel embarrassed for the child and for the display of their own emotions during the disintegration stage. Perhaps as an attempt to deal with these feelings of "Where do we go from here?" teachers at this stage ask a lot of questions. Typical are "What is bothering you?" "How are you feeling?" "Why are you acting like this?"

The action steps at this stage are to continue to maintain restraint and to issue clear, direct commands. You may want to release the hold you have on the child, but resist this inclination. The child still needs to be restrained physically while attempting to gain composure emotionally. It is best for the child to feel secure physically, so that all energy can be devoted to emotional integration. Reassure the child that you will release him/her in a few minutes. It is important to issue clear commands to the child so that the child has some direction as to how to behave. For example, "Billy, I want you to sit down at your desk," or "Katie, stop crying," or "Jeannette, hold your arms tight."

3. *Verbal Stage:* The student is now ready to verbalize his emotions and vent some of his feelings in a controlled, linguistic manner. Usually the student will ask to be let go and become more coherent in speech. He/she will start to describe what happened preceding and during the disintegration stage.

Teacher reaction is one of relief, giving advice, or trying to apologize for what happened. There is a general sigh of relief once the teacher realizes everyone is going to be okay, or that the damage inflicted will not become worse. There is a need to tell the student what to do and how to act in the future when things like this happen. Some teachers feel the need to apologize for becoming so physical with the student.

Action steps at this stage are to lessen the restraint and to listen carefully to what the student is saying. Once the student starts to verbalize what has happened and talk, you can be assured that some measure of self-control has been attained. It is safe to remove the restraint and allow the student some personal distance to regain composure. Ask the student how he/she is feeling. You will need to use the active listening skills described in Chapter 2 to understand and to communicate your understanding of the student's feelings to the student. The most essential of the active listening skills at this point are reflection of content and reflection of feeling.

4. *After-Shock Stage:* There is always some negative reaction from the student following integration or composure of feelings. Sometimes the student will pull away from you and maintain a distance greater than usual for talking. Sometimes students will swear at you once you have let them go. They may want to get in the last shot and throw an object or make a hostile or antagonistic remark to another student.

Teachers' reactions may be renewed anger, hurt, or guilt. A teacher may wonder if the restraint was lessened too soon. They question and have doubts about how integrated the student has become since the disintegration stage. They feel hurt that the student has fooled or betrayed them. They may even feel guilty for allowing the student to say or do things in the after-shock stage.

The action steps you take during this stage are not usually directed at the student. Let the student give his/her parting shot. You have won the confrontation because you have calmed the student down. What the student has done is natural self-correcting behavior which restores his/her own feelings of dignity and potency. You should, however, direct some attention to the students who may have witnessed this out-of-control behavior. Explain to them to the best of your ability why the student is upset, what happened during the disintegration and composure stages, and what will happen now. Students who observe all this behavior may have feelings similar to yours. They need to talk it out also. Ask them if they have questions about what happened or if they agree or disagree with your actions.

Their responses will give you feedback as well as give feedback to others as they attempt to give meaning to the event.

Action Technqiue 3: Controlling. Infrequently considered during confrontations with out-of-control behavior, is the control of the crowd witnessing the event. Many times teachers are so involved in the management of the student acting out that they fail to notice or devote energy to the management of other students. These students, witnesses to your confrontation, can provoke or escalate the acting out behavior by making simple remarks or throwing objects at the student. You need to control the crowd.

The best technique to control a crowd is to give directions or tasks to specific individuals at various points in the crowd. Start in the middle of the crowd; pick out a student and ask that person to go get the principal. Then turn your head and address a specific student on the right flank of the crowd. Ask this person to get you a drink of water or something. Then turn to the crowd's left flank and pick another specific student to accomplish a specific task, like moving the desks out of the way. Address the students by name. If you do not know the names, then address the students by what they are wearing or how they look. For example, "You there in the red pants and white sweat shirt, please move these chairs back."

By giving directions to individuals in different areas of the crowd, you are creating a dynamic by which you are telling the crowd that you aware of who is in the crowd and that you know what the students are doing. You are telling the crowd that you are holding it responsible for its behavior. Crowds are more likely to become negative and antagonistic if the individuals think they can remain anonymous.

If, by chance, a student or two become hostile in the crowd, single them out for special attention. If you know their names, remind them that you know who they are and what they are doing. Tell them you are busy now restraining a student, but when the event is over you will devote your full energy and time to them. If you do not know who the student is, tell the student that you know what he/she is wearing, what color it is, and remind them of the possibility that in your school building you will definitely meet him/her again and when you do meet, you will devote your full energy and time to their paying the consequences of provoking this confrontation.

Action Technique 4: Explaining. A public outburst of out-of-control behavior by a student requires a public follow-up of the results and consequences. In any school building where a student displays such volatile behavior, word spreads quickly. While many students might relish the idea that a student went wild with you, when the event is over they expect you to follow-up with some action. This follow-up will also become part of the story which will be retold for years. Students need closure to an event of this magnitude. They expect the student to pay the consequences and they should be allowed to know what that involves.

One suggestion is to post the student's name on the bulletin board citing the consequences of the action. In your building it may be a suspension, or a referral to the Committee on the Handicapped, a change of class, or even compensation for damages. Whatever the consequence, it should be fair, consistent with past policy, and a logical reaction to the out-of-control event.

CASE STUDY

The following is an example of an actual incident with a student who went out-of-control. References to the action steps mentioned earlier are to the right.

This incident took place in the cafeteria during lunch period. Charlie was angry because Eddie had teased him and had stolen some money from his desk.

Charlie stared at Eddie for a full five minutes while Eddie went through the lunch line to get his food. Observers said Charlie was tracking Eddie like a cat. Charlie's body was rigid and he was reportedly breathing shallowly. Only his eyes moved.

The two teachers on duty failed to see Charlie's early warning signals, rigid body, and shallow breathing prior to the explosion. Had they detected the signs of anger, they might have been able to prevent the rage that followed.

Once Eddie was sitting down with his lunch, Charlie made his move. He picked up a chair over his head and charged at Eddie, screaming profanity as he ran.

This is the disintegration stage.

One of the teachers screamed back at Charlie and tackled him before he reached Eddie. The other teacher started swearing at Charlie and helped to hold down his legs. Eddie, meanwhile, moved away from Charlie but started screaming profanity back at him.

Emotional reactions from teachers were aggressive in nature.

Eddie also reacted with emotional aggression, but did not react with physical aggression.

The first teacher who was holding Charlie's arms down against the floor, told Charlie to calm down and asked Charlie to trust him to resolve the conflict. Charlie responded by saying he was going to kill Eddie.

The first teacher here was reacting with emotional fear, fear perhaps that Charlie had lost trust in him. The teacher had to be sure their relationship was intact. Physical restraint on the floor was appropriate. Charlie never heard the teacher's question about trust. Charlie was still consumed by rage.

The second teacher told Charlie to be quiet and then told him over and over again that he was on the floor, thrashing his arms and legs about, sweating around the mouth, and that had torn his pants at the zipper.

The teacher here mirror-imaged Charlie's behavior.

After a few minutes Charlie closed his eyes and his body relaxed. One of the teachers asked if he was all right and had calmed down. The other teacher asked Charlie to lie still and take some deep breaths.

This is the composure stage.

The first teacher reacted emotionally with questions. The second teacher gave clear, simple commands.

One student witness yelled out for Charlie to kill Eddie. Another said Eddie should get Charlie while he was down.

Charlie asked to be let up. He said that he was angry at Eddie because Eddie took his money. One teacher said he was sorry he had to sit on Charlie and hold him down.

After Charlie was released he stood up and swore at Eddie who was still standing across the room. One of the teachers escorted Charlie across the room and upstairs to the principal's office. While they were going up the stairs, the teacher told Charlie that he was disappointed at hearing the last swear word.

The following day a notice appeared that Charlie was suspended for five days.

Teachers ignored the crowd, which was trying to escalate the situation; they should have used crowd control techniques.

This is the verbal stage. Charlie verbalizes his feelings and the teacher reacts emotionally by apologizing.

This is the after shock-stage. Charlie gets in the last shot be swearing at Eddie.

The teacher reacted emotionally by being angry at Charlie's remark.

This is the explaining state. Everyone knows that Charlie received the fair, logical consequence of his out-of-control behavior.

Figure 3–1 summarizes the confrontation strategies.

Seven Operational Guidelines

1. Low Threshhold for Disruption
2. Negotiate
3. Deal with That Observed
4. Express a Clear Goal
5. Use Direct Language
6. Have a Bottom Line
7. Follow-Up

Three Nonverbal Techniques

1. Body Congruence
2. Personal Space
3. Body Positions

Four Verbal Techniques

1. Confront Deletions
2. Confront Distortions
3. Confront Generalizations
4. Confront Cop-outs

Threats

Classroom Confrontation

Out-of-Control Students

Prevention Techniques

1. Rating
2. Mirror Imaging
3. Talk Behind the Back
4. Pacing Vocally
5. Walking
6. Feel Blocks
7. Relaxation

Action Techiques

1. Ignoring
2. Restraining
    1. Disintegration Stage
    2. Composure Stage
    3. Verbal Stage
    4. After-Shock Stage
3. Controlling
4. Explaining

Figure 3–1. *Review of confrontation strategies.*

REFERENCES

Bandler, Richard, and John Grinder. *The Structure of Magic I*. Palo Alto, California: Science and Behavior Books, 1975.

Bramson, M. *Coping with Difficult People*. New York: Ballantine Books, 1981.

Maurer, Richard E. "The Effect of Postural Congruence on Client's Perception of Counselor Empathy," *Journal of Counseling Psychology, 30,* April 1983, 158–163.

Pease, Kenneth. "Attitudes in Linguistic Communication: A Further Study of Immediacy," *Journal of Personality, 40,* 1972, 298–307.

Woolfolk, Anita E., and Douglas M. Brook. "Nonverbal Communication in Teaching," *Review of Research in Education, 10,* E. Gordon ed. Washington, D.C.: American Educational Association, 1982.

Instructional Strategies

The purpose of this chapter is to help you recognize, refine, and develop a working knowledge of fourteen different instructional strategies. These strategies have been identified in educational research as instrumental in improving classroom discipline and student academic performance. Most teachers have developed their own teaching strategies based on past experiences in school and a knowledge of their own personal needs. Many of you may recognize your own strategies in some of those described here. Most of you will be able to identify others which you have found effective. The common bond, which is recognized in all of these fourteen strategies, is that they provide a high level of structure for lesson planning, but a flexibility of response during instruction.

It is suggested that as you read through these strategies, think about examples of how you use them, in which classes, and when during the day they are most appropriate. In cases in which you don't use them, where could you begin to experiment? An observational checklist called "The Teacher Performance Assessment Instrument" is located in the Appendix and provides an easy method of observing the fourteen strategies described in this chapter.

HOW TO ALTERNATE MODALITIES

You can perceive or learn about something only through the five senses: seeing, hearing, touching, smelling, and tasting. These are the only ways in which you can receive information. The five sensory modalities are the keys to the cognitive functions of the brain. Examples of how you may use them in your classroom are listed below:

- *Seeing (visual learning):* Student views the chalkboard, reads, watches a demonstration, or views a movie.

- *Hearing (auditory learning):* Student listens to your descriptions or your lecture, hears a story, or listens to a tape.

- *Touching (tactile learning):* Student touches objects, writes notes, or writes letters.

- *Feeling, a form of touching (kinesthetic learning):* Student learns by engaging in a physical activity such as role-playing or making something. Student also learns by the emotional response (feels good) something may trigger.

- *Smelling (olfactory learning):* Student learns by recognizing odors and making associations to past knowledge.

- *Tasting:* Student learns by putting objects into mouth.

Many of you use all five keys when teaching; however, most do not. In fact, the higher up you go in education, the fewer modalities that are employed by the teacher. At the elementary level students are constantly learning through a variety of modalities, but at the university level learning takes place primarily through the visual and/or auditory modalities.

None of us learns using only one modality. We use them all in various combinations. Listening to a lecture, we may hear the words but we also watch the speaker's movements or diagrams, which help clarify the message. We all, however, have developed one modality to use as our primary gatherer of information. It is the key we employ to initially learn something. For example, there are those who like to learn or learn more quickly by reading; those who learn by listening or talking; and those who learn by doing. We all know people who hate to read; those who love to talk; those who need to fidget with something; those who need a diagram or picture before they can fix something. What about students? They are no different. They each learn most quickly and efficiently in a different fashion. Some are primarily visual learners, some auditory, some tactile, and some kinesthetic. Research (Barbe and Milone 1980) has shown that about thirty percent of students have a visual modality strength; twenty-five percent an auditory modality strength; fifteen percent a kinesthetic modality strength; and about thirty percent a multiple modality strength.

Figure 4–1 on pages 130–131 provides a rough idea of the strength of each of your modalities. Listed are ten incomplete sentences and three ways of completing each sentence. Check the statement which is most typical of you.

Two concerns immediately arise in the classroom with relation to modality learning. The first is the compatibility of the primary learning/teaching styles of the teacher with the learning styles of the student. For example, in many schools there are teachers whose primary teaching strategy is the classroom discussion. These teachers could be described as auditory learners. If a student in the class has a primary learning strategy in a different modality, such as reading, he/she may have difficulty sitting through forty weeks of this teacher's class. Or, if a teacher encourages students to take a lot of notes during class (tactile learning) and a student dislikes writing but needs to talk about the subject to understand it, there is a problem of incompatible learning styles. If a student is learning disabled, meaning, has a learning deficit in one or more of the modalities, he/she is going to have serious problems in the class of a teacher whose primary teaching method is in the area of this student's weak modality.

The second concern is with overload. Too much input in one modality tends to cause that modality information processor to become overburdened and eventually phase out. We all have been at lectures or at a church service where the most interesting subject area is being discussed only to find our mind drifting away from the speaker. We look around the room at others, we daydream, we doodle, we may read our program, we may even sleep. What is happening is that the auditory cognitive system is overloaded and the brain switches to another modality channel to find stimulation. Some research has shown that after ten minutes most average adults tend to start shutting down the overloaded modality. This overloading is best illustrated by the process many of us use to go to sleep. Some like to read or watch TV in bed before sleep as a way of relaxing and beginning to feel sleepy; others listen to music, and still others like a warm bath or shower.

What is the solution to these concerns of incompatibility and overload of modalities? *Alternate the modality you are teaching with.* By

1. My emotions can often be interpreted from my:
   ( ) Facial expression
   ( ) Voice quality
   ( ) General body tone

2. I keep up with current events by:
   ( ) Reading the newspaper thoroughly when I have time
   ( ) Listening to the radio or watching the television news
   ( ) Quickly reading the paper or spending a few minutes watching television news

3. If I have business to conduct with another person, I prefer:
   ( ) Face-to-face meetings or writing letters
   ( ) The telephone, since it saves time
   ( ) Conversing while walking, jogging, or doing something else physical

4. When I'm angry, I usually:
   ( ) Clam up and give others the "silent treatment"
   ( ) Am quick to let others know why I'm angry
   ( ) Clench my fists, grasp something tightly, or storm off

5. When I'm driving I:
   ( ) Frequently check the rear view mirrors and watch the road carefully
   ( ) Turn on the radio as soon as I enter the car
   ( ) Can't get comfortable in the seat and continually shift position

	Visual	Auditory	Kinesthetic
6. I consider myself:	( ) A neat dresser	( ) A sensible dresser	( ) A comfortable dresser
7. At a meeting I:	( ) Come prepared with notes and displays	( ) Enjoy discussing issues and hearing other points of view	( ) Would rather be somewhere else and so spend my time doodling
8. In my spare time I would rather:	( ) Watch television, go to a movie, attend the theatre, or read	( ) listen to the radio or records, attend a concert, or play an instrument	( ) Engage in a physical activity of some kind
9. The best approach to discipline is to:	( ) Isolate the child by separating him or her from the group	( ) Reason with the child and discuss the situation	( ) Use acceptable forms of corporal punishment
10. The most effective way of rewarding students is through:	( ) Positive comments written on their papers, stick-ons, or posting good work for others to see	( ) Oral praise to the student and to the rest of the class	( ) A pat on the back, a hug, or some other appropriate physical action
Total number of boxes checked:	—— Visual	—— Auditory	—— Kinesthetic

Figure 4–1. *Find your modality strengths.**

*Walter B. Barbe and Michael N. Milone, Jr. *Find Your Modality Strengths* (Honesdale, PA: Zaner-Bloser, Inc., 1980).

alternating modalities you can reach the different types of learners in the class and you can keep their brains stimulated. For example, rather than lecturing for forty minutes, lecture (auditory) for ten minutes; have the students do silent reading for ten minutes (visual); have a discussion about the lesson for ten minutes (auditory/kinesthetic); and give a written quiz on the material for ten minutes (tactile). Most classroom lesson plans can be broken down into different teaching modalities. Some subjects can only be taught using a variety of the modalities. Science classes usually have lectures (auditory), reading (visual), note taking (tactile), and lab assignments (kinesthetic). Most special education teachers need to alternate modalities continuously if their students are to understand the material.

Below are listed some suggested learning activities for each of the four modalities used in the classroom. The smelling and tasting modalities are rarely used by themselves, so they are not inlcuded.

Visual

- Have students do silent reading.
- Have students view a map, graph, or diagram located on the board. (This is far point visual study.)
- Have students view the same material on ditto sheets on their desks. (This is near point visual study.)
- Have students work at a computer for a short period.

Auditory

- Use class discussions for short periods. Brainstorm ideas, opinions, solutions, characters.
- Ask one student to comment on another's statement.
- Lecture for a short period without students taking notes.
- Ask students to stand up and summarize for the class what they have just heard.

Tactile

- Ask students to take short notes on your lectures.
- Ask students to work in their workbooks.
- Ask students to write a reply to a letter or a statement of another student.
- Ask students to draw a four-block cartoon sequence using stick figures to summarize the lesson so far.

Kinesthetic

- Have students act out certain roles, vocabulary words, historical events.
- Have students act out different parts of an object, such as an engine or an ear.
- Engage students in simulation games which require them to use the lesson material presented, such as a courtroom scene to illustrate aspects of the law.

Examples of how you might incorporate alternating modalities into your lesson plan are listed below. Remember, it is not necessary to switch modalities for the sake of switching. If your lesson is progressing well and you observe students are on task you may wish to continue teaching in the same modality for a longer period.

Reading: Ask students to read short passages aloud, randomly changing readers. Have students silently read three paragraphs, then engage the class in a discussion of the passage. Ask the class a question, then have them skim the reading to find the answer. Next have the students read a passage and make up two questions for the rest of the class. Ask students to draw a picture summarizing what they have learned in the readings.

Films: Describe what to look for in the film about to be seen. Show the film for ten minutes, turn on the lights, and have a short five-minute discussion or question-and-answer period about what was seen and what will happen. Show the film for another fifteen or twenty minutes. Again stop the film for discussion, role play, note taking, or picture drawing.

History: Give a brief lecture on the period to be covered and the objectives of the lesson. Assign roles to each student or group of students. Have each group prepare a short biographical sketch of the role. Students will need to read and discuss the role with you and others. On each day give a short lecture of the period being researched to provide background information. Ask students to prepare notes. At the conclusion of the research, hold an assembly where all the characters meet to discuss an issue. For example, Knights at the Round Table, Dewey at Tokyo Bay, Kennedy on the Cuban Crisis.

Science: Present a cross section of the human ear, lecture on the functions of each part. Ask students to repeat in unison the parts of the ear and their functions. Ask students to make a drawing of the diagram cross section for their notebook. Have students assume positions in the room and physically walk another student through the "ear" to illustrate the transmission of sound.

HOW TO ALTERNATE INSTRUCTIONAL FORMAT

Consider for a moment what your classroom looks like. Are all the desks in rows, one behind the other? Do you have tables in your room and do you use them for instruction? Are there individual learning centers for students? How your room is organized affects how you teach.

There are four primary ways teachers teach:

- In a *large group format,* the teacher instructs all of the students in the class at the same time. There is no other learning going on at the same time as the teacher's delivery (lecture, note taking).

- In a *small group format,* the teacher instructs small groups of students at an assigned place (reading in groups, math teams, lab projects).

- In the *seat work format,* the students work independently at their desks without direct teacher contact (silent reading or workbooks).

- In the *individualized format,* the teacher works one to one with a particular student.

Most elementary school teachers use all four formats every day. Most high school teachers use only one—the large group format—all day.

Which is the best format? They all are needed at different times for different types of students. Like alternating modalities, if you alternate instructional formats, you can keep the student stimulated and learning the same material in different ways. The time to switch instructional formats is the time when a certain number of students are off task or no longer paying attention to the lesson. By shifting formats, you are forcing them to stop daydreaming and start thinking.

Below are listed criteria or warning signals which you can use to help determine when to switch formats.

Large group lesson: You are appropriately using this format if at least 90 percent of the students are maintaining eye contact or are on task with you. If, however, you can count that more than 33 percent of the students are not on task or maintaining eye contact with you, then you are teaching at a student frustration level. It is best to switch formats or modalities.

Small group lesson: If the students in these groups are getting at least 80 percent of the work correct, you are using this format appropriately. If a student starts to miss or starts to make errors in more than 20 percent of the work, then it is time to switch.

Seat work format: When students get 80 percent of the work correct you are making appropriate use of this format. A 20 percent error rate indicates time to switch.

Individualized format: Ideally this format should have the student performing on task 100 percent of the time. However when there are errors they should be very low (three errors every two minutes) since you are instructing, explaining, and demonstrating at the student's appropriate academic level.

Procedure

Here are examples of using alternating instructional formats within three different class situations.

A 45-Minute Class

Large group	(8 minutes)—	Daily review, homework correction, reteaching of areas of difficulty.
Large group	(10 minutes)—	Development of new material, explain, demonstrate, and illustrate.
Small group	(10 minutes)—	Seat work assignments given to apply and practice new material.
Individualized	(7 minutes)—	Review strengths and weaknesses of comprehension, answer questions, reteach areas of difficulty.
Large group	(10 minutes)—	Review of lesson, assign homework, answer last-minute questions.

Heterogeneous Groups

In schools where students are grouped heterogeneously and varying levels of ability exist in one class, the following organization of instructional formats is excellent to use for high academic performance. Let us assume there are three ability groups in math. Students in groups I and II can be given seat work, while those in group III could be in a small group format at your desk. Here you could use flashcards or single problem solving to review, reinforce, or introduce a new concept very simply and effectively. The students in group III sit with their backs to the rest of the class so they are not distracted. Some students in groups I and II could be working on math problems through the use of audio tapes and phone headsets. At the end of ten minutes group I comes up for small group format, group III starts seat work, and group II divides into pairs to correct the seat work completed. At the end of another ten minutes all groups switch again.

General Instruction

Using the three-group separation again, it is possible for you to do most of your instruction in a small group format. In reading, for example, group I could be allowed to find a book or magazine to read from your class shelf or the library, group II could be given seat work such as completing worksheets on yesterday's lesson, and group III could be in small group format being instructed in new material. After a period all groups switch. In this case you are making only one preparation but delivering it three times.

Figures 4–2 through 4–5 show how you might place the students' desks for certain types of instructional formats.

The arrangement in Figure 4–2 is excellent for large group lessons. Every student can be seen, students can speak to one another, and the teacher can move freely throughout the room.

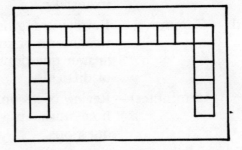

Figure 4–2. *Large group lesson format.*

The arrangement in Figure 4–3 lends itself to small group lessons. Groups of four students can work on a project without interfering with others.

The arrangement in Figure 4–4 is best for seat work where each student needs a private area in which to complete work or read silently.

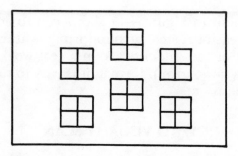

Figure 4–3. *Small group lesson format.*

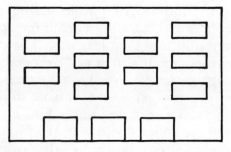

Figure 4–4. *Seat work lesson format.*

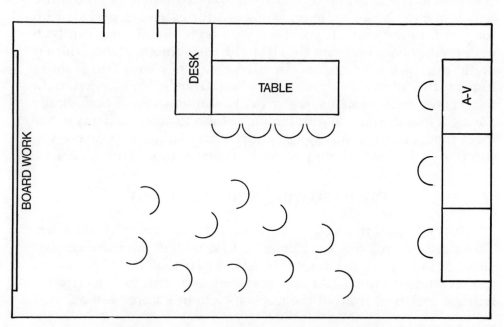

Figure 4–5. *Arrangement for all three formats.*

The arrangement in Figure 4–5 allows you to accommodate all three formats very easily. A small group format is at the table in front of you and the rest of the students are in a seat work format. If you want to move into a large group format, it is easy to turn the desks to face the front of the room.

HOW TO VISUALLY SCAN

You should be in a position to view activity and maintain personal eye contact with all students. This should decrease the students' tendencies to "mind-drift" while acting as an effective retentive teaching tool. Visual scanning encourages personal contact while enhancing community and joint learning. The scanning process can be reinforced with comments such as "We need you in this...," "You're drifting, hang in there," "We have to stick together here." Scanning also enables you to observe and evaluate student response to the concept being taught. You can determine how many students are on task or maintaining eye contact with you. If a high percentage are no longer paying attention, then it is time to either switch modalities or instructional format. Never sit where some of the class activity occurs behind you. It is best to find a location against a wall where the entire class is visible. Never write on the board for extended periods with your back to the class. If you turn your body slightly, you can both write on the board and view the class with ease. Another tactic which is useful is to pick four students in a large class of twenty-five to thirty students that sit in the following locations: front, left side center, right side center, and back. By just visually scanning them periodically during a lesson, you will give the impression to other students in the room that you are scanning the entire class. Although your eye will sweep over the room, it only needs to focus on those four students.

HOW TO PROVIDE ACTIVE MOVEMENT

It is essential that you move around the classroom as you teach. There are two reasons for this. The first is that you increase your visual scanning scope. Research* has shown that the high rate of teacher-student eye contact and questions and answers come from a triangle region in front of the teacher. Note in Figures 4–6 and 4–7

---

*M. Koneya, "Location and Interaction in Row and Column Seating Arrangements," p. 272, *Environment and Behavior, 8* (1976). Copyright © 1976, Sage Publications, Inc. Reprinted by permission of Sage Publications, Inc.

(you are at the area marked T) that the back and most of the classroom sides are out of this triangle region. Teachers generally do not look at or answer a high rate of questions from students in these areas outside the triangle. By moving about the room you shift your perceptual triangle and, as noted in the figures, those students formerly excluded now enter the region where they will be looked at and asked questions of more often.

Another reason to move about the room is that it allows you to touch students and to praise them individually for the work they are doing. Both touching and offering praise are correlated with increased classroom performance. Often, if a student is talking during a lesson, just walking near and placing your hand on the shoulder is enough to get him/her back on task.

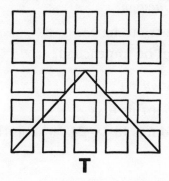

Figure 4–6. *Active movement diagram.*

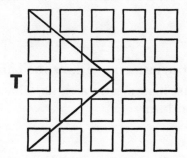

Figure 4–7. *Active movement diagram.*

HOW TO DO ACTIVE QUESTIONING

Active questioning is one of the most efficient means of keeping students on task. A question every two or three minutes is an excellent rate for helping students pay attention and for getting some feedback on student comprehension levels. It seems, however, that very little talking in a classroom is related to questions and answers. Research has shown that in most classrooms someone is talking two-thirds of the time, and two-thirds of that time it is the teacher, and two-thirds of the talking the teacher does is giving directions.

There are, however, at least six different types of questions which can be asked.* Each of these types requires a different type of response from the students.

The Fact Question

- Who was the President during the Civil War?
- What is the capital of New York State?

The Comprehension Question

- Who did the villain try to harm?
- How can a President be impeached?

The Application Question

- Show me how to boot this disk.
- Given the family room is 18′ × 24′, what is the area of the room?

Analysis

- Why did the Dutch lose their colonies to the English?
- What options does the President have for dealing with a large budget deficit?

Synthesis

- What are the major arguments of how the earth was formed?
- Given this hero's past history and actions, what will happen if his best friend turns on him?

Evaluation

- What will happen to the number of students buying lunch in the cafeteria if we reduce the prices?
- If the level of acid rain increases 10 percent, what immediate effects on wildlife will be seen?

---

*D. G. Armstrong; J. J. Denton; and T. V. Savage. *Instructional Skills Handbook* (Englewood Cliffs, NJ: Educational Technology Publications, Inc., 1978) pp. 103–105.

By using fact and comprehension type questions you can increase the amount of information a class can learn about a particular subject. Being able to apply this information through application type questions reveals that the class has developed a higher or working level of knowledge about the subject. Answering the last three types of questions, analysis, synthesis, and evaluation, requires abstract reasoning ability. A student who can master these responses has made the information his/her own by being able to "network" it to pieces of other information already known. This networking ability is a sign of sophisticated human intelligence at work. What more could you ask?

There are seven effective methods of asking questions.

1. When you ask for information, put the student's name at the end of the question. "Name two major cities in the Midwest, Mary." This way you are potentially putting all the students on call because the question may come to them. All the students will not only be paying attention, but will also start to think of the answer.

2. Have students answer each other's questions. For example, "Do you agree or disagree with Mary's answer, Paul?" This way, students are the critical processors of the information. *You can escape from being the main talker,* and everyone is forced to think about every question.

3. You should call students on a random basis if you want to keep students' attention spans active. As we discussed earlier, movement around the room assures that you are changing your perceptual triangle and more students have a higher chance of being called on.

4. If you wish to check student comprehension of the material, calling on students in a sequence is helpful. Ask the first student in the first row to talk for fifteen seconds on the subject. The next student has to pick up where the first left off. This student should talk for another fifteen seconds and so on until the last student in the last row is given an opportunity to contribute to the data base the class is building on a particular subject. You will be surprised at how much knowledge this questioning technique can generate.

5. Use an auditory closure technique for fast-paced questioning. For example, "The atmosphere or mood this writer is trying to create is one of depression and...and what, Robert?" or "The two chemical elements in oxygen and hydrogen are...what, Ron?"

6. Wait three to four seconds before you respond to a student's response to your question. Most teachers wait on the average of only one second. If you wait a bit longer the following will result:

- The length of students' responses increases.
- The number of unsolicited but appropriate responses increases.
- The confidence of students in their responses increases.
- The number of students failing to respond decreases.
- The number of students who interact and exchange information increases.
- The number of responses from low achieving students increases.
- The number of questions asked increases.

7. Call on nonvolunteering students as well as volunteering students. If the nonvolunteering student does not know the answer, move on quickly to another student with the question. Once an adequate response has been given, then return to the first student who did not know the answer and ask the same question again. It is important that the student be able to comprehend the information and know that you are holding him/her accountable.

HOW TO RESPOND TO LESSON INTERRUPTION

It was explained in Chapter 3, "Confrontation Strategies," that an excellent preventive technique is to keep a low threshold for disruption. Anything which interrupts what you are doing should be first recognized and then dealt with. If the disruption does not cease, continue to keep your lesson on hold and apply one or more of the techniques on confrontation described in Chapter 3.

There is a story circulating in one school that a math teacher kept right on teaching his lesson despite the fact that a ten-foot window blind fell to the floor. While students moved away from the windows and the dust was astir everywhere, the teacher kept on talking. It must be assumed that the teacher really was as confused as the students as to what to do. Hoping things would settle down as quickly as possible, he did what he was taught best to do—he kept on teaching. Meanwhile, the students enjoyed the excitement and, as the story goes, were oblivious to what the teacher was saying.

In this case, the teacher should have followed the rules listed here:

1. *Stop* the lesson.
2. *Tell* the students what you want done.
3. Explain *how* you want it done.
4. *Wait* for results.
5. *Tell* the class to get back on task.
6. *Continue* the lesson.

If he had followed these rules, this is what would have happened immediately after the blind fell.

TEACHER:	(Closing his book and putting the chalk on the chalkboard tray) Now boys and girls, I want you all to close your books and those of you in the aisle near the window march up to the front of the room. Bring your books. Move quickly now. Bring your books, remember.
RICH (a student):	As Chicken Little says, "The sky is falling…the sky is falling!" (Students laugh)
TEACHER:	We'll laugh about this in a minute, right now I need you eight near the windows near me.
EVELYN (a student):	Well it beats doing math.
TEACHER:	Hold your remarks until everyone is settled. (Waits for the students to assemble near him) Okay, now, I want each of you, one by one, to return to your desk and get your chair. Let's do this in silence, everyone. We'll comment on it soon enough. (He waits until each has a chair) Now please sit along the front of the room and let's hear from those who have a comment or two.
STUDENTS:	(A number of students laugh, crack jokes.)
TEACHER:	Well, it certainly is exciting enough here. Now that we are all awake, let's get back to work. Open the book to page 37 and, Kay, start reading.

In classrooms of less effective managers, the following four distractions occur at a very high frequency with predictable consequences to the lesson.

Distraction	*Consequnce*
1. Out-of-seat students	• Students are disengaged. • Students distract and disengage others. • Students model inappropriate behavior.
2. Excessive noise	• A cause and effect relationship is formed. Once you stop to deal with the noise-makers, then other students become distracted and make more noise.
3. Call-outs	• Students force you to respond to them, rather than you controlling the process. • Students who are the loudest and most assertive get most of the attention. • Usually out-of-seat behavior increases proportionately to the frequency of call-outs. Those who cannot get your attention verbally will try to do so physically.
4. Delays in beginning	• Students become engaged in their own personal agenda from which it is difficult to disengage them. • Students learn it is okay to come late, eat food, or clean desks during instruction time.

The key to handling lesson interruption is to deal with it as if it were the most important thing of the day. Once students realize that you will devote so much energy, time, and personal interest to their disruption, you can be sure that they will seek to avoid prolonged involvement with you. The time spent dealing with disruptions will be reduced drastically. Listed below are methods to deal with lesson interruption:

1. Exaggerate the disruptive behavior. If Billy starts making clicking noises, ask him to stop, and if he continues say something like this: "Bill, you make great clicking noises. Could you come up to the front of the class and show the class how to do it?" In most cases, Billy will be so embarrassed that not only will he not stand in front of the class, but his disruption will stop immediately.

2. In cases where the disruption occurs outside the classroom, such as a window washer doing your windows or a lawn mower going back and forth outside, stop the lesson and ask the students what to do. Here, you are recognizing the disruption and are still in control by asking the students to recognize it and come up with alternatives to deal with it. By fielding the questions, answers, and comments, you are showing the students that you still are in complete control.

3. Physically change your position when you deal with a disruption. For example, if Marylou and Elizabeth are talking, simply stop what you are doing, move away from your desk or the board, and ask them to pay attention. This physical change communicates a nonverbal message that the talking is serious enough to disrupt your instruction, that you are ready to employ other confrontation methods if they don't comply, and that you are switching roles, from instructor to manager.

4. Enforce formal time by flicking the lights or clapping your hands. This signal means all students are to be seated, quiet, and must raise their hand if they have a question or need to be recognized.

5. Put a stack of review questions on a desk near the door. As students enter the room, each one picks up a sheet and sits down to work immediately. You can stand near the door and provide verbal encouragement and extra directions to those few students who have the most difficulty getting settled.

HOW TO ALTERNATE ROLES

All teachers use these three following different roles when they are in a classroom:

Manager role: You give directions and manage the organization of the class and the flow of the lesson (collecting homework, taking attendance, and so forth).

Instructor role: You deliver information concerning course content; you explain and illustrate (lecturing, demonstrating).

Peer role: You become actively involved in the learning situation with the students; you discover and learn together (going on field trips, attending assemblies, sharing personal experiences).

There is no question that all three roles are important. However, it is the second role, the instructor role, which allows you to get information into a student's head most efficiently. It is the role you were trained for and that for which you are paid. The manager role is adopted to deal with tasks concerning the logistics of the classroom operation. Many teachers report that this role is the one which gives all the grief and headaches. The peer role allows you to step out of your information-giver role and learn with the students.

It is not uncommon in a class where the teacher has forty minutes to deliver a lesson to find him/her spending five to seven minutes at the beginning and five to seven minutes at the end of the class collecting homework and absence notes, recording attendance, answering questions, and passing out equipment and books for the lesson. Twenty-five percent of class time can be spent just getting organized. Students also have learned to cue the teacher near the end of the period that it is time to switch roles from the instructor to the manager. Five minutes before the end of the period you often find that students start to cap their pens, close their books, stop answering undirected questions, comb their hair, and fidget more in their seats. Most teachers respond to these cues unconsciously and either start to summarize, demand more attention, pass out homework assignments, or just give up instructing and retreat behind the desk.

Here are a number of ways to reduce the time spent in the manager role:

1. *Use formal and informal time.* Formal time is when students must raise their hand to make a comment or be called upon. Informal time requires less structure and a student may call out the answers and comment freely. If a class discussion starts to reach a noise level at which you feel it is disruptive to the lesson, or if a number of students are talking but not participating, rather than spend a lot of energy to control the noise level, just announce to the class that it is "formal time." You will

find that you have immediate control as the students calm down. Other forms of announcing that formal time is being instituted can be turning the light switch off and on, clapping your hands loudly, or closing the blinds.

2. *Start and end the class with seat work.* When students come into the room have a worksheet prepared or a ditto projected on the screen which has problems or questions about yesterday's lesson. Students must enter the room and start to work immediately. In schools where students must come from other classes, this procedure allows you to have students entering over a five-minute period without disruption or a high noise level. Five minutes before the end of the period ask students to write answers to a few questions or solve a few problems. This way students are working up to the time the bell rings and you are free to handle individual cases. All papers are collected and counted toward the grade. As you pick up the papers or as students hand them to you, place A + on the papers of students who did not talk and A − on the papers of those who did.

3. *Help students organize themselves.* Require students to keep a notebook in which he/she can insert notes, sheets you hand out, graded papers, and other essential information. Provide students with an outline of how homework papers are to be written. Such items as name, date, page numbers, and problems should follow a consistent form.

4. *Collect collateral.* The chief problem for many teachers is providing students with pencils or lunch money. Collecting debts is a major task. Require that students give you something which is important to them to hold until the debt is paid. For pens and pencils collect a shoe or scarf. At the end of the assignment you can be assured you will get your pencil back. Collateral for lunch money can consist of such items as jewelry, toys, combs, or other personal objects.

5. *Use quizzes to calm students down.* If the class is particularly excited or disruptive, and announcing "formal time" does not work, then give a short quiz. One or two questions is often enough to get the students back to the lesson objective. You have saved yourself a lot of time and energy by not having to cope with the excitement.

HOW TO TEACH TO FORM THE IMAGE
OF WHAT IS BEING TAUGHT

It is essential that lessons be planned so that the end result is one where students are able to form an image of what is being taught. This process is one where the specific information you are giving them comes together as a whole and is clear. If students are unable to form an image, they can get lost in all the information you are providing. For example, in discussing the American Revolution, students may lose sight of the essential purpose of the event in their own lives if they become bogged down memorizing dates or names of the major battles. While this information is important, it has little meaning without students having a clear overview or a perspective of how it fits into other pieces of information.

A number of techniques may be used to help in the process of enabling students to form an image. Many of these techniques require students to engage in functions of their right brain hemisphere.

1. Ask a student to summarize the material by asking him/her a leading question. "I would like you to point out the importance of two things about the Revolution which we studied today, Rebecca."

2. Have the students draw a picture (tactile modality) of a major concept covered in the lesson.

3. Ask the student to summarize in one or two sentences a particular lesson you have just taught.

4. Ask students to create, infer, give an opinion, or reorder the information present. For example, "What is another way of diagramming this information?" or "What do you think will happen next based on these facts?"

5. Ask students to use imagery to visualize or create internal images of the event, person, or problem being discussed. For example, ask students to close their eyes and visualize two historical people talking, the movement of chemical elements, the functions of a computer program, or the action of certain vocabulary words taught during a particular lesson in one or two sentences.

HOW TO REDUCE TRANSITION TIME

Transition time is defined as the amount of time it takes a classroom of students or an individual student in the room to come to task. For example, if you tell your class to put their spelling workbooks away and take out the math homework, you will have a certain amount of time spent in making the move. This time is, for all practical purposes, "instructional down time." Now, some down time is important because it gives the students a break in the instructional pace. You also have an opportunity to gear down before the next lesson. Problems arise when the down time is too long and students start their own agenda to fill the void. Students discuss what they are going to do after school, they may look out the window, and in some cases even act out with each other. Methods to reduce this class transition time are indicated below:

1. Tell the class they have a certain time limit to make the transition. For example, "Okay, class, you have one minute to put your readers in your desks and get your coats. Those who cannot do it must wait an extra five minutes before being dismissed. Okay, begin!"

2. If many students are out of their desks working on projects in the classroom, first ask everyone to put away what they are doing and sit at their desks. Once everyone is sitting, inform them of the next activity. This step-by-step method reduces classroom noise, efforts by students to wander about the room, and possible disruptive behavior. In the younger grades students could have difficulty remembering a multiple command.

3. When students are coming in from other classes, first have everyone sit down. Now that you have control, inform those who have absence notes, permission to leave early, or homework; those who need to get books from the shelf; and those who need to talk to you to move about. No other student should be away from his/her desk. It is easier to manage the transition time of a few students that that of the entire class.

4. Students in the class you have rated to be particularly poor in their transition time need to be given extra structure. You could inform the class as to which student has the poorest time for transition and that the class needs to encourage this individual to move along. Peer pressure is hard to resist.

5. The pressure to make a quick transition could be applied to students in another way. Reward students, the first five perhaps, who make a transition the fastest.

6. Give a warning that a transition is about to happen. "Okay, class, in five minutes we will be ending our social studies period and beginning math period." For a particular student, it might be a good idea to individualize this warning. "Okay, James, in five minutes we will be switching from social studies to math. Can you handle a quick and quiet transition?"

7. Once the transition is about to be made, get everyone's attention. "I want everyone to close their social studies books now. That means everyone, Timothy. We will not make a move until everyone is ready with a closed book and quiet."

The other transition time occurs when an individual student enters the class while instruction is going on. A student may be late to class or may have been at a special class, the library, or cafeteria. The student entering a room from another activity needs to know what is going on in this room. It has been noticed that as a student enters the room he/she could spend a lot of time and energy in off-task behavior. He/she could wander over to his/her desk by an indirect route; speak to others; pick up objects; search for paper, books, and pencils. The best method to reduce this student's transition time is to verbally give him/her a command as soon as he/she enters the room. For example, "Stevie, we are on page 97 in the math book. Please get your book and sit down at your desk." You may need to reinforce this verbal command by moving over to Stevie's desk as a way of showing him where he is to go. Meanwhile, your instruction is not drastically affected because most of your time is spent in the instructor role. While brief commands are given to Stevie, you can easily keep the remaining students on hold and quickly return to the lesson pace.

HOW TO REVIEW WHAT YOU TEACH

Review is the most neglected instructional technique. Studies have shown that the average student needs ten reviews of a concept before the knowledge is retained in long-term memory. Special education students with learning problems need 2,500 reviews of a concept before they know it. Remember, you are teaching to form an image. Students need to know how things fit together. Don't assume they see any connection between what you did this week and what was covered the week before. Some suggestions for review:

1. Have a weekly review each Monday for twenty minutes. Focus on skills and concepts covered the previous week.

2. Have a monthly review every fourth Monday. Focus on skills and concepts covered since the last monthly review.

3. Have a vacation review the day the class returns from an extended vacation break. Focus on skills and concepts covered since last extended break.

4. Have a report card review the day after report cards go home. Remind students what they learned before the report card and how it will be connected to the new material.
5. Review the following:
- The main idea
- The objectives of the lesson
- The important points in the lesson
- The summary and application ideas you have mentioned as the lesson proceeded

The following ideas are helpful in setting up a review program:
- Charting (For example, the chart in Figure 4–8 on biology provides students with efficient information recall.)
- Exhibits
- Games/Contests
- Drills
- One-Minute Oral Reports
- Posters
- Story Telling
- Workbook Assignments
- 20 Questions

	Digestion	Reproduction	Excretion	Aging
Humans				
Cows				
Pigs				
Fish				
Earthworms				

Figure 4–8. *Sample of recall chart.*

HOW TO POST A SCHEDULE

Every morning a schedule of the day's activities should be posted. If you teach only a forty-minute class, then post what you are going to do for this time period. Don't assume students know where you are going with the lesson. What may be logical to you and sequentially outlined in your plan book is a mystery to most students. Some students do not care to know what is going to happen. They live moment to moment and enjoy the mystery of surprises. These students need to have their time structured. They need to be shown that planning brings coordination and movement toward a purposeful goal.

Students need to know what is expected of them. To help them organize their learning time and to help foster that sense of lesson clarity that is needed to form an image of the subject matter, a weekly class activity chart is useful. (See Figure 4–9.) Each student should receive one of these prepared activity charts on Monday. As the week progresses they can turn the work in to you and after you have corrected it, either place a grade or check off the outcome block to indicate the completion.

Use your chalkboard to keep students continuously informed of what is to happen during the class period. Outline the lesson, state the purpose of the lesson, break the lesson into a time schedule. Figure 4–10 on page 154 is an example of a schedule for a forty-minute English writing class.

Figure 4–11 on page 155 is a summary schedule (Rosenshine 1982) for an elementary math class. This schedule, when implemented in over twenty classrooms, had such a profound effect on student achievement in only two-and-a-half months that it is considered important to teaching math. In addition to the selected time segments, this schedule also allows for alternating modalities and alternating instructional formats. Both of these strategies were discussed earlier in this chapter.

HOW TO POST CLASS RULES

The rules for your classroom should be established within the first week of school. Many teachers welcome student input in forming the rules. This is appropriate especially at the upper grade levels. However, you should post rules which you want followed. These rules are not open to negotiation. They should be few, fair, and relevant to

ACTIVITY CHART FOR _____

_____   _____
Subject   Week of

Day	Objective	Book	Pages	Outcome
Monday				
Tuesday				
Wednesday				
Thursday				
Friday				

Figure 4–9. *Weekly class activity chart.*

the primary functions of the classroom. The consequences of violating these rules should be clearly stated. During the first week explain to students why you have developed these rules and why they may be different from some of the more general rules in the school. When you post these rules, write them in large letters and display them where even the students in the back of the room can read them. Here is an example of a list of rules from a middle school teacher.

1. No food or gum.
2. No profanity.
3. No leaving the room without a pass.
4. You must bring a pencil.
5. During formal time no one may be out of his/her seat.

In terms of classroom management you need not expend a great deal of energy to enforce these rules. For example, if a student is chewing gum you merely have to say to the student, "Mike, rule number one." The student knows exactly what you mean, knows the consequences, and in four words you have confronted Mike. You only had to step out of your instructional role for a short time.

If students complain about your rules, remind them that you are the teacher and why you developed them. You should recognize that some rules may cause inconvenience to students, but emphasize that these rules are yours and you are the boss. One teacher, who is very sensitive and caring to student needs always tells his students when they complain about the rules that his classroom is not a democracy, that he is the boss, that the rules should be obeyed. When students complain that his rules are more strict than other teachers' and that he is unfair, he reminds his students that life is unfair and that they had better get used to it. Not surprisingly, this teacher is extremely popular with his students. For many students coming from a dysfunctional home where no rules and few social boundaries exist, a classroom that is well defined with regard to routine and rules is quite welcome. For most students, the establishment of clear rules helps them structure their behavior and develop self-discipline. Those

---

Lesson: How to write a business letter.

9.20—Examples of correct business letter forms.
9:30—Students write their own return addresses and letter
       heading to a firm.
9:50—Comparison of correct form to student heading.
10:00—Review of correct form.
10:05—Homework.

Figure 4–10. *Sample schedule of an English class.*

Each Day Review (First 6 to 8 minutes except Mondays, when it should be twice as long)
1. Check previous day's work, including workbook and homework activities.
2. Reteach where there are errors.

Presenting New Content/Skills (20 minutes)
1. Provide overview of skills and concepts.
2. If necessary, give detailed or redundant instructions and explanations.
3. New skills are being phased in while old skills are being mastered.

Initial Student Practice (15 minutes)
1. Provide a high frequency of questions and overt student practice (from the teacher and from materials).
2. All students have a chance to respond and receive feedback.
3. The teacher checks for understanding by evaluating student resonses.
4. There should be a success rate of 80% or higher during initial learning.

Feedback and Correctives (Recycling of instruction if necessary, 5 minutes)
1. Feedback to students, particularly when they are correct but hesitant.
2. Corrections are provided by simplifying questions, giving clues, explaining or reviewing steps, or reteaching last steps.
3. When necessary, reteach using smaller steps.

Independent Practice (10 minutes)
1. Provide uninterrupted seat work.
2. Need to establish accountability procedures to ensure student engagement during seat work.
3. A 95% success rate ensures that application of skill is firm and automatic.

Review Weekly and Monthly (Reteach if necessary)

Figure 4–11. *Sample schedule for a math class.*

students who choose to test your class rules and your resolve will find that you are well prepared to discipline them and confront them with techniques learned in Chapters 2 and 3.

Listed here is a suggested procedure to use during the first week of school in terms of helping you implement your school rules. More effective managers tend to spend a great deal of time during this week setting the stage, so to speak, for students to follow the rules.

- Present your rules the first day of class and concentrate on the procedures and consequences for the first five days.
- Explain the rationale for your rules for the first five days.
- Practice necessary procedures such as lining up, going to the bathroom, turning in papers, formal and informal time.
- Ask for and give feedback to the students about how well or poorly the procedures are being followed during the first week.
- Rules and their implementation procedures need to be taught to students. Like any subject matter, the process involves presentation, review, reminder, application, and correction.

Sometimes students ask to become involved in setting the classroom rules. You may or may not agree to this principle. However, if you do believe students should have a voice in setting their own procedures, you may want to make a class project out of the event. It is not recommended that you start the school year off without rules. As was mentioned in Chapter 1, the absence of rules will cause anxiety and present major management problems. Later in the school year you may wish to have students write their own rules. Figure 4–12 shows how a class of middle school students comprised their own class commandments.

HOW TO PRAISE STUDENTS

Studies have shown that we all think we are the best at what we do. Even when experiences prove us wrong, we are remarkable at self-deception. We will blame anything, anybody rather than admit our incompetence. The corollary of this is that we all need to be reminded of our greatness. We need to be praised. One salesman says it well, "Praise the customer, what she is wearing, what he said, what they did, and they will believe anything you tell them after that."

Class Commandments:
Student Rights and Responsibilities

1. All students should try their best.
2. Students should be allowed to sit near their friends as long as they do not disturb the class.
3. Students should be allowed to make occasional comments to friends, as long as they do not disturb the class.
4. Students should be pleasant to the teacher.
5. Students should not steal from one another.
6. No student shall have the right to ridicule another.
7. Students shall be allowed to leave class for the restroom, as long as they return in a reasonable amount of time.
8. Students should be allowed to help one another.
9. Students shall be considered innocent until proven guilty of such acts as cutting, copying, or cheating.
10. Students shall have the right to free expression of ideas.

Teacher Rights and Responsibilities

1. Teachers should not subject students to abusive language or physical abuse.
2. All teachers shall be fair, understanding, patient, and kind.
3. Teachers shall keep in mind student workloads in assigning nightly homework.
4. No teacher shall embarrass a student in front of classmates or make him feel stupid.
5. Teachers shall not treat students as infants, but as young adults.
6. A teacher shall not penalize a student for coming two or three minutes late to class.
7. Teachers and students should try to be friends.
8. Teachers should like kids.
9. Teachers should explain clearly what they are doing in class.
10. Teachers should not preach or try to impose their own personal values.

Figure 4–12. *Sample class rules.*

Students have egos also. They need to be told they are doing well, are correct, are liked, are good, and are even appreciated. You should praise a particular student for work, for an answer, for thinking ability, or for behavior. Reinforce answers even if they are close to being correct. If you see a student doing something right, recognize it. One study, which counted the number of critical remarks and the number of positive remarks teachers made to students, found a lopsided ratio of six negative remarks for every one positive. The ratio should be exactly the opposite. Positive reinforcement is so much more powerful than negative reinforcement. A good example of this can be seen in many elementary school classrooms in which a student will do almost anything to gain a gold star stuck to his desk.

Many teachers of older students feel praise in an unnecessary fringe benefit students do not need to achieve. They believe the report card grade is sufficient reward. If a student needs to be told he/she is doing well, then it can be done when written comments are put on returned work, quizzes, or lab reports. Classrooms where students excel, however, are places where praise takes place all the time. Not only do teachers praise students, students praise students as well. Listed below are some examples of how to increase the number of positive remarks to students.

1. Stand at your classroom door as the students enter. Single out a student or two and as they enter put your hand on their shoulder and tell them how good it is to see them, what fine clothes or jewelry they have, what a good mood they are in.

2. Prepare a list of your students and plan on making a special remark to each of them over the period of a week. For example, "Judy, I have noticed you coming to class early each day this week and doing extra work. How productive you are!" or "My that haircut you got is nice!" Record student comments for use when you plan on a second round of praise.

3. Place a star, flower, school emblem next to the names of those students present each day.

4. During the middle of a lesson mention the names of those students who are working particularly hard.

5. Plan a weekly, monthly, quarterly, annual hoopla celebration of student achievements. Plan that everyone gets an award eventually for something. In one special education class everyone received an award in June. These ranged from best grades, best

attendance, best reader, to even best drawings. Everyone won something.

6. Hold a class or even a school-wide meeting the first few minutes of each morning to recognize birthdays, community events that students participate in, sports performance, classwork achievement. Push the hoopla, sing "Happy Birthday," say "hip, hip, hooray," sing "For He Is a Jolly Good Fellow." Students at the higher grade levels may say it is silly to do such things, but nonetheless they love the fuss.

HOW TO GIVE HOMEWORK

Students who must do homework increase time on task. The more time spent studying, studies show, the higher the achievement of students. But not only must homework be assigned and done by students, it must be collected and scored by the teacher. Homework which is not corrected becomes busywork for students. There is little evidence to show that students will work efficiently on homework if they know the work will not be looked at. Homework which is not corrected immediately for the next day's lesson loses its importance to students. Students need to receive follow-up the next day. Errors made on homework need to be known to students if they are not to repeat them on the next day's work and if they are not to become confused on the next sequence of a lesson.

All homework should be given at an independent level of instruction. It should be review work only. If you present new work to a student, he/she may get frustrated, probably do the majority of it incorrectly, and most likely over a period of time stop doing homework. Remember, repetition is important to learning. Homework increases the amount of time you can spend helping a student review the work you have previously taught.

There are times when a student refuses to complete homework. You may have tried every technique you know to make this student submit the required assignments. In cases such as these there is one technique which is quite impossible for the student to ignore. Make it a privilege to do homework at home. Students who habitually do not do their homework must first complete it after school. Only after demonstrating that they can complete it after school for five days will they have earned the right to do it at home. Most schools run late buses, so with parent approval, a homework clinic can be easily implemented. You now have eliminated the choice to do or not do homework.

It is important to remember that homework fulfills a need of the parents as well as of the student. Most parents see the work as a sort of individualized assignment through which their child learns more. It allows them to spend time with their child and even help him/her with the work, which increases the sense of individualization. The homework gives parents an insight into your course objectives. It helps them form the image of the subject as well.

Listed are some helpful tips on giving homework:

1. Give homework every night of the school week. Some teachers don't give homework on Fridays; however, on this night students have an extra two nights to complete the work. Also by giving homework on Friday, you increase review time by 20 percent.

2. Fifteen to twenty minutes of homework a night is considered average. Judge the importance and difficulty of your work using this measure.

3. All students should be given homework. If homework is assigned as a class or school-wide policy, then it should be given to everyone.

4. Parents should be told to expect homework every school night. If there is an exception to this rule, you will write them a note explaining why. Have homework signed each night by parents, not for them to correct, but for them to be aware of it and help to ensure that it gets done.

5. Teach students how to do homework. This includes the format in which you like the papers completed and the method of how you collect and correct them. Help each student plan the method of completing the work, where in their house or apartment they should do it, at what time of the night, what distractions should be eliminated, and so on. The best policy is for students to do the work the same time and same place each day.

6. Have students save their returned corrected homework, keeping a special file or notebook for it. Award students at the end of the week, month, year who have the heaviest collection of papers.

Homework needs to be a collaboration between parent, student, and teacher. To help you in this process it is suggested that you provide parents at back-to-school night with a copy of your course objectives and some information about how you run the class. Some suggested ideas to include in this handout are:

Grading policy

Homework—when, how much, and how it is to be collected

Class projects

Class field trips

Due dates for special papers

When extra help is offered

Class supplies students will need

Special class rules

How and when a parent can reach you

Course textbooks, workbooks, etc.

Figure 4–13 summarizes instructional strategies.

1. Alternate modalities.
2. Alternate instructional format.
3. Visually scan.
4. Provide active questioning.
5. Do active questioning.
6. Respond to lesson interruption.
7. Alternate roles.
8. Teach to form the image of what is to be learned.
9. Reduce transition time.
10. Review what you teach.
11. Post a schedule.
12. Post class rules.
13. Praise students.
14. Give homework.

Figure 4–13. *Summary listing of instructional strategies.*

REFERENCES

Anderson, Linda M.; Carolyn M. Evertson; and Jere E. Brophy. "An Experimental Study of Effective Teaching in First Grade Reading Groups," *The Elementary School Journal, 79,* 1979, 194–223.

Barbe, Walter B., and Michael N. Milone. "Modality," *Instructor Magazine*, January 1980, 44–47.

Baur, Gregory R., and Darleen Pigford. *A Survival Guide for the Junior High/Middle School Mathematics Teacher.* West Nyack, New York: Parker Publishing Company, 1984.

Gage, Nathaniel L. *The Scientific Basis of the Art of Teaching.* New York: Teachers College Press, 1978.

George, Paul, and Gordon Lawrence. *Handbook for Middle School Teaching.* Glenview, Illinois: Scott, Foresman, 1982.

Good, Thomas L., and Douglas A. Grouws. "The Missouri Mathematics Effectiveness Project: An Experimental Study in Fourth Grade Classrooms," *Journal of Educational Psychology, 71,* 1979, 355–362.

Good, Thomas L. "Teaching Effectiveness in the Elementary School: What We Know About It Now," *Journal of Teacher Education, 30,* 1979, 52–64.

Painting, Donald. *Helping Children with Specific Learning Disabilities.* Englewood Cliffs, New Jersey: Prentice-Hall, 1983.

Rosenshine, Barak. "Content, Time, and Direct Instruction," *Research on Teaching: Concepts, Findings, and Implications,* P. Peterson and H. Wazberg, eds. Berkeley, California: McCutchon, 1979.

Rosenshine, Barak. "The Master Teacher and the Master Developer," paper presented at the American Educational Research Association's annual convention, New York, New York, 1982.

Shulman, Lee S., and Gary Sykes, eds. *Handbook of Teaching and Policy.* New York: Longman, 1983.

Wayson, William W., and Thomas J. Lasley. "Climates for Excellence: Schools That Foster Self-Discipline," *Phi Beta Kappan, 65,* February 1984, 419–421.

Peer Consultation: A Strategy for Professional Growth

Peer consultation is a method in which teachers team up to help each other learn new discipline, management, and instructional techniques. Essentially, it requires that teachers be trained to observe, analyze, and provide feedback to each other on what it is they are doing in the classroom that works and what it is that does not work in terms of promoting positive behavior. Peer consultations are not evaluations in the administrative-contractual sense of the term, but are a sharing of ideas, techniques, implementation difficulties, and optimism among teachers. A secondary gain from this strategy is that it directly promotes staff morale. One cannot participate in this process without feeling more positive and confident about one's teaching performance and the performance of others in the school.

RATIONALE

One question you may ask yourself is "Why do I need to observe other teachers in order to learn new teaching techniques?" Another form of the same question may be "What can I possibly learn from others who work in essentially the same conditions I do?" The answer to both of these questions is that the best resource you have to grow professionally are the colleagues in your building. They, like you, are the best in the business. They each have teaching skills they are masters at and, like you, they rarely share these skills with each other. In the teaching profession, classrooms are often sacred quarters into which colleagues rarely venture. Often, looking to a colleague for help is viewed as a weakness, not as a sign of professional competence. Being a professional means, however, that one does seek out colleagues for advice and criticism. Other professions such as medicine, psychology, law, and sports instruct their members to do just that and to consider peer consultation as a professional responsibility.

One of the assumptions associated with being a professional is that you possess a certain repertoire of techniques and competencies in an area which distinguishes you from others not in the area. The more competencies you possess or have a working knowledge of, the more professional you are. If you goal is to become more professional then you should consider where and from whom you can find additional training and observe additional techniques.

There are three traditional sources of teacher training—graduate education courses, school district inservice workshops, and direct supervisor coaching. If you consider each of these you will discover limitations as to the degree and frequency of your exposure to new competencies. Many teachers have been removed from formal graduate education for a number of years. So much new information on learning, psychology, and curricula has been developed that teachers removed from formal education can become outdated in some professional skills. Many researchers report that school inservice courses are not effective in changing a teacher's classroom performance. The reasons offered often center around the lack of relevant training content, teacher initiative, follow-through, and money, as well as the general belief that a school environment is a complex array of organizational systems and subsystems which exist to resist change. The third area of teacher training mentioned previously—direct supervision or coaching—suffers from the fact that the number of qualified supervisors does not even come close to fulfilling the need. Some estimates put the supervisor-teacher ratio at one supervisor to every 200 teachers. If you can find a supervisor in your building who is competent enough to know instruction, psychology, and curricula and is free enough from administrative duties to devote many hours to you, then you are indeed fortunate.

So where can you learn new teaching skills? Learning from other teachers in you building is not only logical but certainly more efficient than any other single teacher training method. When used in conjunction with graduate education courses, inservice workshops, and/or supervisor contact, peer consultation can be an extremely powerful tool to train, retrain, and generally improve your teaching skills. There is clear evidence in the research that demonstrates that the use of peer consultation does improve classroom performance. One study reported that only five percent of the teachers who participated in a staff development program which included theory presentation, a demonstration, and teacher role play of a specific skill were able to retain this skill after two months. However, when peer feedback was added to the training component, the rate of those who retained the skill after two months jumped to ninety-five percent (Joyce et al 1981).

FIVE-STEP PROCEDURE

The process of peer consulting involves the implementation of a five-step procedure (Goldhammer 1969):

1. A pre-observation meeting with another teacher
2. An observation of that teacher performing in the classroom
3. An analysis of your observation notes
4. A conference with the teacher to report what you observed
5. A post-conference analysis of your effort.

The Pre-Observation Conference

The reason for this short meeting is for the exchange of some preliminary information needed for the observation and for the reduction of anxieties. You should discuss with the teacher you are about to observe the following points: (1) the time of the observation, (2) the type of class, (3) the particular curriculum content, and (4) special difficulties with individual students. As a result of this discussion, you should be able to develop a sense of the teacher's goals for the lesson and some initial feeling about how this teacher instructs and disciplines. It is best to avoid giving advice at this meeting about the dos and don'ts of instruction.

The reduction of anxieties is needed because no matter how experienced you are at the teaching business, the presence of a colleague—especially someone you do not know well—in your room will produce some tension. As the potential observer, you may feel a bit uneasy observing someone outside your subject, grade, or experience area. You will probably be concerned about giving a good impression and writing a "good" consult. One of the easiest ways to lessen this tension is to just state how you feel about being involved in observing the other teacher's class. Being a bit tense, however, is normal and should not affect the observational or analytical skills necessary to do a peer consult. Remember, you are competent at your job and so is the person you are observing. No one will see your peer consult except the teacher observed.

After you have been involved in a number of peer consultations, your pre-observation conferences may take a more focused direction. You may want to look for specific teaching behavior, such as the type of movement you engage in when you teach or the type of confrontation you use with a particular student. You may want the observer to give you some feedback on changes in discipline, management, or instructional techniques you are trying to implement. In summary, this preliminary meeting sets a contract that you will observe at a certain time and place and the teacher will instruct the students in a certain subject. The groundwork has been laid for the most important aspect of the process—the conference.

The Observation

The first thing to remember about observations is that they are not evaluations. You are not looking for "good" or "bad" teaching behavior, but rather what does and does not work in the classroom. The focus is on what the teacher does to promote positive discipline and student learning. In some instances you are looking for specific behaviors; in other cases you are trying to discover the gestalt or the general feeling in the room which contributes to these core conditions.

Looking at a teacher teach is somewhat like looking at the back of an open watch case. Like the mechanism which runs the watch, a teacher's performance in front of a classroom is a complex interrelated set of behaviors, the sole purpose of which is to perform a task—to instruct the students. Unlike the watch movement, however, the teacher also contributes the human element of feelings and emotion into the works. Combine these teacher behaviors with the complex interrelated behaviors of individual students and you can imagine the rich field of human interaction which occurs in every classroom.

There is so much going on in a classroom that one can easily observe too much and not really see anything. The stimuli can just overwhelm one's senses. The written description below is that of a class observation by a teacher who saw so much that he could not be specific enough to convey what the teacher did during the lesson.

8:34 A.M.   Sue is working on pronouns.

- Teacher very well organized
- Teacher has excellent bulletin boards
- Room is divided re: subject area
- Teacher is supportive of student needs
- Students are involved and understand lesson
- The lesson is light and humorous

A clearer description of how this teacher disciplines and instructs students might be included in how this teacher "organizes" her material and how this contributes to the instructional delivery plan. Other possibilities might be a description of how the bulletin boards are used in the room in terms of instruction; which instructional format works best in which divided subject area; how the teacher "shows support"; and how being "light and humorous" contributes to the students being "involved" and "understanding the lesson."

If your task in the peer consultation process is the discovery of which teaching behavior works and which does not, then it is essential that your perceptual focus be disciplined enough to facilitate this discovery. Two observation instruments have been developed to assist in this process. Both can be located in the Appendices along with a description of how to use them. A brief outline of each is given below:

1. *The Teacher Performance Assessment Instrument.* This instrument provides a frequency count of fifteen teaching behaviors which have been identified in educational research as contributing to increased student learning. The observer looks for and records the occurrence of one or two of these behaviors during the observation period. This instrument is popular with those teachers completing their first observation because it is relatively easy to score and limits the observational task to specific areas of teaching.

2. *The Global Scale of Teacher Performance.* The purpose of this scale is to obtain an overall perspective of what happens in a classroom in terms

of teacher-student behavior and how this behavior contributes to a high level of student learning. The focus is not on specific teacher behavior as it is in the "Teacher Performance Assessment Instrument" but rather on how certain teacher behaviors combine to produce certain desired classroom results. These results or effects are the fostering of four core conditions which exist in every classroom.

Most observation periods need be only ten to fifteen minutes long. You will accumulate enough data in this time to be able to provide the teacher with excellent feedback. For your initial observations, decide before you go into the classroom which criteria you are going to observe. When you gain some experience with the two instruments you may want to choose criteria to observe after you have entered the classroom and have had a chance to observe the dynamics. If you do choose the criteria beforehand, it is not necessary to tell the teacher what you are going to observe.

A few things need to be remembered concerning the use of these instruments:

1. They are not meant to be used to evaluate teachers. Their purpose is to help the observer limit his/her perceptual field so some critical effective teaching behavior can be discovered.

2. These instruments do not pretend to measure nor do they contain criteria of all the effective teaching behaviors of every teacher who performs in a classroom. No one instrument has been developed nor probably could be developed to accomplish this task. Both these instruments attempt to help the observer discover *some* of the teaching behavior found to be effective.

3. The results obtained from each of these instruments should not be considered the end product of the peer consultation process. Rather, it is the feedback that the observer gives to the teacher which is most important.

Examples of how each of the observation instruments can be used are provided here:

Observation 1. Mike used the "Teacher Performance Assessment Instrument" to observe Dan's middle school honors English class. Twenty-eight students were in the room, and Dan was teaching a large group lesson on how to discover metaphors in short stories. At the pre-observation conference Mike was made aware of the lesson content, but decided not to inform Dan as to which criteria he was going to observe. Mike chose the following criteria:

6 Frequency Count of Active Questioning

9 Rating of Lesson Clarity

10 Duration of Transition Time

The checklist items in Figures 5–1 through 5–3 demonstrate how Mike recorded the observation. In order to record the transition time, Mike was careful to be in the room at the start of the period. The total length of this observation was 15 minutes.

---

6. Frequency Count of Active Questioning
   The number of times a teacher asks questions to individual students.

   Record Number: _____ / / / / / / _____

   Time Span Measured: _____ 3 minutes _____

   Ratio of Questioning (Number::Time): _____ 2::1 _____

   Comments: Dan uses questions to provide feedback on student

   comprehension level.

   He also puts names at the ends of questions to keep students

   awake and processing each question. For example, "How

   would you describe the character, Mary?", "Give me another

   word for enlightenment that would fit here, Wendy" and

   "Challenge that thought, Brad!"

Figure 5–1. *Sample from "Teacher Performance Assessment Instrument."*

Observation 2. Using the "Global Scale of Teacher Performance," Randy observed Cynthia during a reading lesson. Five middle school students were seated at a small table with Cynthia. The remaining

9. Rating of Lesson Clarity

The rating the observer would give the teacher's lesson presentation in terms of clearness of purpose, effect, and relationship to previous lesson material.

a. Observer's direct rating of clarity of presentation:

_____ Explained how the lesson

1   2   3   4   ⑤   fit into yesterday's work.
unclear   clear   very
                        clear

b. Observer's rating of the students' understanding of the clarity of lesson's presentation.
(Ask two students the following question: "Do you understand what has been taught?" or "Why are you doing this?")

_____

1   ②   3   4   5
unclear   clear   very
                        clear

Manny–2: "I don't know, he wants me to learn this."

Terry–5: "It follows the study of poetry we did last quarter

....It is needed for the exam....Imagery that is

....part of our experiences."

Comments: There is a wide range of student understanding for

why this lesson is being taught.

Figure 5–2. *Sample from "Teacher Performance Assessment Instrument."*

students were seated at their individual desks, writing in their workbooks. The small group lesson was to teach the five students how to pronounce new words by sounding them out.

At the pre-observation meeting Randy had a chance to hear about the lesson and to read Cynthia's plan book. Prior to entering the room he decided to look at what Cynthia does to deliver the information or

10. Duration of Transition Time
    a. The amount of time the class as a whole takes to change
       from one lesson (e.g., math) to another (e.g., reading).
       Measurement from teacher's instruction to initiate a change
       to time it takes the last student to come to task on the new
       lesson. _____ 7 minutes

    Comment on Student Behavior: _The bell for 4th period rang_
    and only 15 of the eventual 28 students were in the room.
    Within one minute the others arrived. You asked students to
    sit down five times, were interrupted after every request by a
    student wanting something (exam, pencil, etc.). It took seven
    minutes into the period before you began the lesson. There
    is a lot of energy being spent here.

Figure 5–3. *Sample from "Teacher Performance Assessment Instrument."*

the content in her lesson plans to the students—in other words, what was her methodology of instruction. While observing, Randy noticed that one of the students at the table had difficulty staying on task. One of the other students tried to get this student back on task. Randy decided while in the room to also record how this student's confrontation was used to establish student relationships.

Randy's written notes demonstrate how to write up an observation using the "Global Scale of Teacher Performance." Since Randy had decided to look at the core condition of the Instructional Task and was interested in Cynthia's delivery plan, he listed "delivery plan" as one criterion to observe. (See Figure 5–4.) When one of the students confronted another in the group, Randy listed "confrontation" as a second criterion under the Student Relationship Core Condition. (See Figure 5–5.) Comments listed on the scale are things he saw, heard, or felt about the lesson observed. The total observation time was fourteen minutes.

The Analysis

After you have accumulated observational data, the next step is to decide which data you are going to share with the teacher at the conference and how. It is important that you reread the observational notes as soon as you can after the observation. Try to develop an image

Teacher Observed: _____Cynthia_____

Date and Time: 11/7 9:00 A.M. Small Group Reading

Observer: _____Randy_____

CORE CONDITION	CRITERIA OR BEHAVIOR OBSERVED	
	Delivery System	
Instructional Task	Reminds them of task, "We are doing sounds." Smiles at Kevin's poor answer. He responds by smiling (nonverbal acknowledgment). Student questioned why vocabulary needed to be studied. Cynthia explained the reason why. Cynthia recognizes different spellings of words. "Good point." Modalities are switched constantly.	
Learning Task		

Figure 5–4. Global Scale of Teacher Performance.

Teacher Observed: Cynthia		
Date and Time: 11/7 9:00 A.M. Small Group Reading		
Observer: Randy		

CORE CONDITION	CRITERIA OR BEHAVIOR OBSERVED	
		Confrontation
Teacher Relationships		
Student Relationships		Felicia tells Chris to pay attention. Cynthia reminds Chris he forgot the answer because he did not pay attention.

Figure 5–5. *Global Scale of Teacher Performance.*

173

of the lesson segment which you observed. What was your overall feeling of what worked and what did not work? Your analysis should only be on the segment of the lesson you saw. Avoid the temptation to extend your data to all of the lesson. It is not valid and probably would not be accepted by the teacher observed.

The next task is to write an analysis of your observation. This will be given to the teacher observed, so you will want to be as precise and careful as possible. It is easy to find the negative; it is harder to look for what works in a classroom. Most teachers have excellent techniques in discipline, management, and instruction which they have learned, seen others do, or which are an extension of their unique personality. Many of these techniques are used unconsciously. The teacher is not aware of how or when the techniques are used. By revealing these positive techniques an observer brings the skill to the teacher's conscious level. Now the techniques can be used more efficiently and powerfully because they can be drawn upon at will by the teacher. His or her repertoire of skilled teaching techniques increases.

If you have observed what you think are things that work well and things that do not work well, it is appropriate to keep your written analysis of positive to negative remarks at a rate of about nine to one. This is especially important for your first few peer consultations. One reason to keep the positive to negative ratio high is that, human nature being what it is, the teacher will remember the negative things said during the conference more frequently and longer than the positive. By keeping this ratio of positive to negative high, there is a stronger chance that the positive skills will also be remembered. Teachers who have been consulting for a length of time often ask the observer to spend more time looking at aspects of their teaching which they know or have learned are not their strong points. The ratio here may be adjusted to five positive to two negative or even to three positive to three negative.

There are three important criteria to consider in writing your analysis. Talk about what you saw; keep your comments to a minimum; and when making suggestions for change, only include those behaviors which you feel the teacher can truly adapt.

1. In your written analysis make a statement about what you saw the teacher do or say. For example, statements such as, "You moved about the room an average of once every three minutes" or, "Your voice tone rises just before you ask a question thereby alerting students to pay attention" are more definitive than statements such as, "There is a lot of activity in your room" or, "You really keep them hopping." Later

in your conference with the teacher it is easier to talk about objective behavior—who did what and when—than about vague statements or impressions. Also, objective data is easily defined, can be verified on videotape or in later observations, and can be changed.

2. Too much feedback on what you saw is like too much of anything—you do not know what to do with it all or where to start. By keeping the number of your statements between ten and fifteen, you can give the teacher sufficient feedback without overloading the conference session. From all the statements you made on the observation instruments, pick those which you feel reflect the essence of the lesson you saw. You may be able to organize them under certain general criteria. Exclude observations which do not support the point you are trying to convey as well as those which seem to be chance occurrences. Write the one or two negative comments at the end of the analysis. There may be instances where you feel everything you observed worked well, so it is not necessary for you to include any negative comments. There also may be instances where it seems that nothing you observed worked well. You may feel embarrassed for the teacher observed. It still is important to look for things that work well, if even only the obvious.

3. If you observe that some of the techniques of the teacher do not work or do not seem to accomplish the goal as efficiently as they could, try to offer some alternative techniques for the teacher to try. It is always difficult to make suggestions for change to a colleague. You should, however, remember that you are not criticizing the lesson, but rather offering better ways of accomplishing the same task. Your frame of reference should be that of a helper or resource person. Most of your colleagues will perceive you in this way, so the task of offering suggestions for change will be easy. In choosing which items to consider for change, determine whether the teacher has the ability, the authority, and the necessary physical means to accomplish the change. For example, if the major discipline problem in one elementary class is a severely hyperactive student who cannot remain seated for more than five minutes at a time, there is probably little the teacher can do to control this behavior over a long period. Perhaps a referral to the local Committee on the Handicapped would be the first necessary step toward helping this child.

One final point about the analysis: It is important that the observer give the teacher a copy of the observation analysis. It is not necessary to provide copies of the observation instruments on which you took notes, although some teachers do share everything. As the teacher receives more and more of these analyses from different peer observers, it may be possible for the teacher to make comparisons and contrasts relative to his or her teaching performance over time. Teachers usually report that their particular teaching strengths are repeatedly seen; and with enough observers reporting the same thing, they even begin to believe that the behavior is a strength. Also, over a period of time these analyses can be used to determine if one is successfully changing any particular teaching behavior.

Analysis 1. Figure 5–6 is an analysis of Observation 1, using the "Teacher Performance Assessment Instrument." Mike decided to write a narrative for each of the points he wanted to cover in the analysis. He used his notes on the observation instrument to provide him with the detail and examples he needed to support his analysis. He decided that he would give Dan only a copy of the analysis that follows, not a copy of the observation instrument used.

Mike met the three criteria necessary for a good analysis. When he made direct statements about the lesson, he usually supported the comments with data or a direct quote from Dan or the students. He kept his comments to a few items he felt were critical. His ratio of positive to negative comments was acceptable at nine to one. The last comment is very supportive, as Mike tells Dan that he wants to help in the planning to reduce transition time. Dan can draw from Mike's teaching ideas as well as from his own as he decides how to handle the problem. Mike also expresses his delight at discovering new techniques. He compliments Dan on how he uses homework to help clarify the lesson and how he uses questions to check on comprehension.

Analysis 2. Figure 5–7 is an analysis of Observation 2, using the "Global Scale of Teacher Performance." It is briefer and somewhat more organized than that of Analysis 1 because it numbers the points to be covered and because it lists the observations under three categories: teaching to form the image, praise, and on-task behavior. Randy decided in writing this analysis that the delivery system Cynthia uses to accomplish the instructional task includes teaching to form the image and praise of students. There are other things Cynthia does as part of her delivery system, such as switching modalities (from auditory to visual); but for this analysis, Randy decided to focus on just these two criteria. He also decided that confrontation was used by both Cynthia and Felicia in order to help students concentrate on the academic task.

Teacher: Dan
Time: 18 Minutes
Scale: Teacher Performance Assessment Instrument

I like the way you summarized last night's homework assignment. You clearly tied it to the ongoing lesson plan and showed how it will help the students understand today's lesson.

The purpose of your lesson on metaphors is very clear. I rated it 5 on a scale of 1 to 5. You told students what you were doing, how you were going to do it, and how this aspect is connected to what you did yesterday.

Students saw the lesson as being clear. The comment by Terry, who rated your lesson clarity as a 5, is an example.

Even students who were not sure about the lesson (Manny, for example) were trying to follow you. I suspect the reason for this is because they have a trust in you as a teacher. You command a degree of respect.

You ask questions to keep students on their toes. For example: "How would you describe the character, Mary?" By putting the question first and the student's name second, you make everyone wonder who is going to have to answer the question. Everyone has to pay attention.

You also use questions to provide you with feedback on student comprehension level. I noticed you would repeat a particular point every time you received an answer which was not correct. You repeated it for the entire class, probably guessing correctly that if one is confused, others in the class are also. Excellent idea!

You ask students to comment on each other's responses to your questions. For example: "Challenge that, Brad!" You help students to consider other opinions, broaden their own, and challenge the thinking processes in general.

You devote an enormous amount of energy to starting your class. You care that students are on task, have their books open to the correct page, and are listening.

Your transition time might be too long. You asked students to sit down five different times in seven minutes. Each time a few would sit down and each time one or two students would interrupt your attempt to gain control. Perhaps we can think of ways to reduce transition time.

Figure 5–6. *Classroom observation analysis.*

Teacher: Cynthia
Time: 10 Minutes
Scale: Global Scale of Teacher Performance
Criteria: Use of delivery system and confrontation to accomplish instructional task; use of confrontation to accomplish teacher relationships and student relationships with other students.

You teach to form the image.

1. At the introduction you said, "We are doing sounds."
2. When switching content you said, "Let's do vocabulary now."
3. When you said the above a student said, "Not again." You reminded them of why vocabulary needs to be studied.
4. You pick up nonverbal cues from students, both facial and tonal, about their confusion.

You praise.

5. When a student gave a different spelling of the word, you said, "Good point." Student smiled.

On-task is important.

6. Felicia told Chris to pay attention, reminded him again to obey. It was important for Felicia that everyone be on task.
7. You spend time but little energy trying to keep Chris on task. Possibly putting more energy into confronting would require less time trying to accomplish this goal.

Figure 5–7. *Classroom observation analysis.*

In terms of meeting the three criteria necessary for a good analysis, Randy did very well. He substantiated most of his observational points with direct quotes from the teacher. He kept his comments to a minimum—only seven points. He decided not to talk about the use of modalities in order to keep the emphasis on these points. He included only one negative, statement 7, so his ratio of positive to negative points was within the acceptable range of experienced peer consulters of six to one. And, finally, his suggestion to Cynthia that she change by devoting more energy to her confrontation is something that he felt she could accomplish. Randy could have provided an example of what he meant in point 7, and it is presumed that during the conference with Cynthia he did. A copy of Randy's analysis, which follows, was given to Cynthia during the conference.

The Conference

The post-observation meeting with the teacher should be held the same day of the observation if possible. One reason for this is that your memory of the lesson observed will be clearer than it will be perhaps a day later. Likewise, the teacher will not have to be held in suspense for too long about what you observed.

The first conference between peer consulters tends to be relatively short, ten minutes or so. Often, the observer can be so nervous about not offending his or her colleague that he or she rushes through the analysis and tries to avoid any discussion about the issues. As teachers gain experience, confidence, and rapport with each other, these conferences can extend for over an hour. The observer and the teacher discuss more, listen to each other more, and genuinely try to offer more assistance to each other. In other words, the more peer consulting you do, the better you will be at it.

The first step you should take before the conference with the teacher you observed is to review your analysis. It is helpful to be sure of the points you want to cover and have clear examples of behavior you would like to report. At the outset of the conference give the teacher a copy of the analysis so it can be followed along. Watch your time limit so every point is covered.

The role you would like to be perceived in is that of a colleague who has skills and knowledge in certain areas which may or may not be helpful. Some teachers may perceive you as an evaluator and others as an expert. The evaluation role evokes a negative anticipation and teachers who perceive you this way may be reacting to critical evaluations they have received previously. They assume that you will be able to see every little thing they did wrong; that you will not understand what they were trying to do; that you are biased; and that you lack the experience to judge them. The role of the expert can be equally perilous. You are perceived as the master teacher who knows everything there is to know about child psychology, education, discipline, and most other teachers' curriculum contents. If you are perceived as an evaluator or an expert, you are in trouble.

To counter these possible perceptions, it is helpful to state right at the beginning the role you see yourself playing. Although it may be acknowledged that you are peer consulting, do not presume it will be remembered at conference time. Remind the teacher you are neither an evaluator nor an expert. Preface your remarks by saying you only saw a segment of their lesson and that is all you are reporting on. Emphasize that your observations are limited by the instrument you used and that you had to eliminate some of the observations in the analysis.

Although you and the teacher are talking about teaching behavior, you should remember that you are also discussing a person's professional career. Most are proud of what they do and how they perform. They need to tell you about it and they need to know you understand the what and how. It is important, therefore, that you listen to the teacher's feelings about teaching. It may be helpful to reread the section on Active Listening in Chapter 2 if you need to practice your skills in how to listen for feelings.

It is not enough to just tell a teacher that certain teaching behaviors do not work well or do not accomplish the set goals. That is like leaving the person high and dry. Try to offer some alternative techniques to accomplish the same goal. If you do not know how to do it yourself, you may want to help the teacher by brainstorming ideas and discussing consequences between yourselves. Other ideas may be to experiment with techniques to see which works best or to visit other teachers who have a reputation for having good skills in this one area.

Drawing from the suggestions for change in the two earlier analysis sections, the following solutions could be discussed during the conference.

CONFERENCE 1

Problem: How to reduce transition time.

Solution 1:   Introduce formal and informal time. During formal time students must be seated and must raise their hands for questions, requests, or movement. During informal time none of the above are required, but students must maintain a classroom learning environment. Switch the lights on and off or clap your hands to institute formal time.

Solution 2:   Immediately upon entering a classroom, a student must pick up a quick quiz sheet on the front desk. These sheets contain review questions from yesterday's lesson. Students have five minutes (or whatever time needed) to finish. All sheets are passed forward on signal and the lesson begins. The sheets are graded and these grades are part of the overall grade. Students who must travel across campus can receive sheets with fewer questions so that everyone has a fair chance of finishing at the same time.

CONFERENCE 2

Problem: How to show more energy when confronting.

Solutions: Raise your voice tone when speaking, shift your place or position in the room before confronting so as to demonstrate emphasis, move closer to the student for emphasis, or move the student to a different part of the room for the verbal confrontation.

The Post-Conference Analysis

After you have had your conference with the teacher, it is a good idea to take a few minutes to reflect on how it went. This reflection will help you understand the dynamics which may have occurred. It also will help you prepare for your next conference with perhaps another teacher. Listed below are some questions which you might ask yourself:

1. Where did the focus on the conference discussion lead?
2. What is the proportion of questions?
   a. Too many   = Avoidance of problem solving
   b. Too many by observer   = Interrogation
   c. Too many by teacher   = Dependency upon observer for answers
3. Does either member's behavior become stereotyped?
   "Let's get it over with."
   "I'm listening but...."
4. Was the analysis done the day of the conference?
5. Were the teacher's plans to change from your suggestion or from his/hers?
6. Did values about education or curriculum affect your judgment about the goodness or badness of the lesson?
7. For the next critique of this teacher's class I will look at.... Why?

NINE IMPLEMENTATION SUGGESTIONS

If you are interested in starting a peer consulting program in your school, it is suggested that you follow these steps.

1. Ask a friend in your building to read this chapter on peer consulting. Discuss with this person the idea of the two of you doing one peer consult with each other. The advantages and problems of becoming involved in this process should be freely explored. Aside from the mechanical issues of when, where, and how, the philosophical value of the procedure should be viewed.

2. If your friend decides to become involved, ask that person to observe you first. Later you can arrange to return the observation. It is important for you to break the ice.

3. Once the consulting round is over, the two of you should discuss whether the process has value to each of you and to others teaching in the building. If the answer is yes, then each of you should arrange to have an additional friend become involved. First have everyone read this chapter, followed by a discussion of its merits and the benefits you and your friend found doing a peer consult. If the two additional friends are interested, arrange to accomplish another peer consulting round. Remember, you must observe the person who observes you!

4. Once this second round of consulting is completed, the four of you should consider involving others. The process can easily evolve so that six teachers are involved, then eight, then ten, and so forth.

5. At some point early in the program (usually after four teachers have been involved), it is important to inform the school building principal of what is happening. At this point you are probably not affecting the procedures of the school by leaving the classroom to do an observation or using teaching time to hold a conference. Once the program involves over four teachers, there is usually some need to adjust schedules, even if only slightly, to accomplish observations and conferences. Ask the principal to read this chapter and then invite him/her to meet with those who have been involved. Discuss the merits of the process as well as the limitations. Ask for support. A peer consultation program can run much more effectively if the building administration is aware of it, supports it, and even adjusts schedules temporarily for the program to operate. At no time should the principal see a peer consultation. Peer consulting is not an evaluation

process and therefore should be kept separate from the administrative-contractual teacher evaluation process. Teachers will become more freely involved if they know no one is reading the peer consults but themselves.

6. At some point during the peer consulting process, you should consider videotaping part of your lesson. Replaying this videotaped lesson with a colleague will allow you to do a joint observation and analysis. Sharing of ideas and specific techniques is much more immediate because aspects of your teaching behavior can be analyzed on the spot. You will be pleasantly surprised to watch yourself being so effective in so many specific ways.

7. A method to involve others in the building beyond your circle of friends is to show the faculty a videotaped teaching lesson of a teacher not known by those on your faculty. Analyze the lesson the same way you would an individual observation, but this time have all the teachers viewing the lesson be involved in the analysis. Some preparation of the faculty would be needed, such as introducing them at an earlier faculty meeting to the process of peer consulting, what you and your friends have done so far, the advantages and disadvantages of the process, and the instruments used in observing. Usually most faculty members will respond positively to this type of activity. You should be able to obtain more volunteers for peer consultation. The more teachers that become involved, the more teaching styles and specific discipline, management, and instructional techniques you will observe and have the potential of adapting for your own use.

8. If the number of teachers involved becomes very large, it may be necessary for the group to appoint one as the coordinator. This is important because it is necessary to keep track of who has observed whom and when and to arrange meetings of all involved. Certain times of the school year are not conducive to peer consulting. These are usually the first and last months of the school year, before vacations, during exam times, and when the administration is conducting yearly evaluations. Also, despite the good intentions of teachers to become involved, it often takes someone to announce when the next round of observations will occur and set a deadline (usually four weeks hence) when they should be completed. Some evaluation of the process should be conducted by the coordinator. It need not be complicated. Such questions as how helpful one felt the conference was to his or her teaching, how effective one felt his or her particular critique was, what observation instruments were used, and what

changes are taking place in one's classroom as a result of the peer consultation would be appropriate.

9. One should view peer consultation not as a substitute for the formal evaluation process conducted by supervisors and administrators; rather it should be a supplement to this and can, in fact, be part of the general supervisory plan of a school administrator. It should not be seen as a threat to administrators but as a supportive gesture by teachers to help each other improve. Some administrators have used peer consulting as one of the objectives a teacher needs to complete by the year's end. The teacher must volunteer to take on this objective and the administrator must agree not to view the written peer consult. A discussion about the process as to what was learned and what was changed in the classroom would provide the administrator with sufficient evidence that the objective was accomplished. There are administrators who mandate that all teachers in their building complete two or more rounds of peer consulting. These are, however, in buildings where peer consulting has been going on for years on a voluntary basis. All new teachers must become part of the process.

PEER CONSULTATION:
EXAMPLE 1

Class Description

This observation occurred in a fourth grade science class. There were twenty-four students involved in a large group lesson discussing the characteristics of cuttlefish—a particular form of mollusk. Each student had a waterlife workbook which was opened to a page describing the cuttlefish. Sophie read out loud to the class a paragraph describing the mollusk. As Sophie read, she continuously asked questions of students, had them underline the main idea in each paragraph, and list important vocabulary words. She drew diagrams on the board, referred to a map of the world's oceans, and showed the different pictures of the cuttlefish. After approximately sixteen minutes she directed the students to form small groups of three and look up key vocabulary words listed in the book.

The students displayed high interest in this subject as they enthusiastically answered Sophie's questions, completed most required tasks in the book, and were able to remember and verbalize information learned from other lessons on waterlife. The pace of the lesson was fast with active participation from most students.

The observer used the "Teacher Performance Assessment Instrument" (see Appendix 1) to rate this teacher's performance. In particular item 1, "The Frequency Count of Modality Delivery System" and item 10A, "Duration of Transition Time" were used. Figures 5–8 and 5–9 show partial copies of the assessment tool the observer completed. The actual ratings are given here in the analysis. Only three comments are made, but they are rich in content. This observer was able to pinpoint what made Sophie's class so dynamic and creative. Comment 2 offered some suggestions to change, but did so in a reflective, nondirective manner.

TEACHER PERFORMANCE ASSESSMENT INSTRUMENT

1. *Frequency Count of Modality Delivery System*

The number of times the teacher uses a particular modality to deliver the lesson content.

Visual— The teacher has the students view material or read silently.

Auditory— The teacher speaks to the class or to a student or has the class hear a recording.

Tactile— The teacher has the students write or draw.

Kinesthetic—The teacher has the students act out or role play the content.

Modality (List Each Used)	Time (Record Duration)
Auditory—read passage, questions, and answers.	Constantly switching modalities during the period.
Visual (nearpoint)— underlining text	
Visual (farpoint)—use of board	
Tactile—underlining	
Kinesthetic—switching from large to small group	

Figure 5–8. *Sample from "Teacher Performance Assessment Instrument."*

10. *Duration of Transition Time*
   a. The amount of time the class as a whole takes to change from one lesson (e.g., math) to another (e.g., reading). Measurement from teacher's instruction to initiate a change to time it takes the last student to come to task on the new lesson. <u>55 seconds</u>

   Comment on Student Behavior: _____
   _____ "Eric is on task." _____
   _____ "Rob is already working." _____
   _____ "Jeannette is seated." _____

Figure 5–9. *Sample from "Teacher Performance Assessment Instrument."*

This analysis was developed within three suggested guidelines. First, the observer talked about what was seen, often by giving examples. Second, feedback was kept to a minimum—only three comments. Third, the item suggested for change is clear and easily implemented by the classroom teacher. A transcript of the teacher-observer conference and a commentary of the dynamics is provided in Figure 5–10.

Conference

Dialogue	Comments
Observer: What a lesson, Sophie, you really know how to create a dynamic, exciting class.	Right off this observer is telling Sophie that she is going to hear positive comments.
Sophie: Well, thank you...I enjoy them.	
Observer: Here, this is what I wrote up. It is hard to capture your magic on paper.	
Sophie: (After she read the analysis) You know, when I	Sophie is initially impressed at how much detail the observer

teach, I just teach. I am not aware that I am doing all this. You saw a lot. The one reason I went so long in the lecture was because you were there. I normally would have switched earlier. You were right. I did lose many of them near the end of the lecture.

Observer: I understand because I was there that you changed your plans somewhat. Also, any stranger to the class makes them behave differently. I understood.

Sophie: Thanks for all the kind words.

Observer: Thank you. I am going to try some of what you do during transitions to make them move faster.

Sophie: Like what?

Observer: I loved how you called out the student's names; for example, "Eric is on task.'

Sophie: Oh yeah. That really does work.

Observer: When do you want to see me teach?

Sophie: Oh, let's try Thursday. This time is best on Thursday.

Observer: Good good.

noted. She acknowledges that these techniques give her a better understanding of her technique. She also feels the need to explain why the observer saw so many students off task at one point.

The observer uses active listening here and reflects back to Sophie the content of what Sophie said. In so doing, she tells Sophie that she did indeed listen.

Sophie acknowledges that the observer does seem sensitive to her feelings.

Sophie is impressed with the fact that the observer is going to copy her techniques.

Observer gives a specific example.

The observer right away reminds Sophie that peer consultation involves a reciprocal visit.

Teacher: Sophie
Time: 20 Minutes
Scale: Teacher Performance Assessment Instrument
Criteria: 1. Frequency Count of Modality Delivery System
          10A. Transition Time

Sophie conducted a large group lesson in science. Each student referred to a workbook and answered questions asked by Sophie on related topics. After approximately 16 minutes, students formed into small groups. Most of the material was new to the students.

1. You continuously switch modalities during the lesson (about every one to two minutes), which creates a very dynamic instructional tone to the class. The students were enthusiastic and excited about relating lesson content to knowledge they already knew. For example:

Auditory: The teacher would read a paragraph aloud, ask students for the main idea, for definitions, and for examples. Students responded informally, but the teacher did direct questions to specific students at all times.

Visual (farpoint): The teacher then would write important vocabulary words, refer to a map, and list examples of mollusks that students gave.

Visual (nearpoint): Students were directed to reread the paragraph and search for important words discussed.

Tactile: Students were then asked to underline the main idea and key vocabulary words.

Kinesthetic: After 16 minutes of the above format the students were asked to form small reading groups (three or four students) and use a dictionary to find the meaning of additional words related to the lesson.

2. After 16 minutes I noticed only five of the students writing words. You also visually scanned and realized more and more students were off task. You then decided to switch formats and immediately brought everyone back on task. With this group, 16 minutes in one large group format may be too long a period. It might have been easier to switch formats earlier and reduce the amount of "down time."

3. When you did switch, your transition time was minimal. Students understood your clear command to move into small groups, knew the procedures to follow, and did so quickly. You accomplished this by touching students, helping to arrange the groups and desks, directing individual students to work areas, and moving up and down and then across the desk aisles. You praised students for being on task by such statements as, "Eric is on task," "Ron is working already." This technique also gave notice to everyone that you were aware of who was on and off task.

Figure 5–10. *Sample transcript*

Post-Conference

The observer noted that Sophie was interested in the conference and appreciated the input. The focus of the conference was directly on the observation. The observer's suggestion that Sophie reduce the transition time was accepted with minimal defensiveness. The observer's feeling is that Sophie was made aware of transition time being too long, but that no particular suggestions to reduce this time were needed because Sophie had excellent skills for this task. The observer will ask Sophie to observe how she handles transition when they exchange roles in the next peer consult.

PEER CONSULTATION: EXAMPLE 2

Class Description

This seventh grade social studies class was a lesson on American government. Twenty-six students were present for the class and each had a workbook to refer to. It was clear that Ed commanded a great deal of respect from his students. The atmosphere of the room was warm and the interest in the subject matter high. There was no time during this observation that a student was away from his or her desk. It was evident that most of the students wanted to work. The pace of the lesson was not intense, so there were time and energy for open discussion and informal exchanges of questions about subject matter. A teaching assistant was present in the room. This person helped the slower students with the reading during the large group lesson. The students who were better readers did not mock or show impatience with those who were slower. They seemed to accept this reality and the fact that the class moved through the work together with everyone keeping pace. This class of twenty-six students was in the performing stage of its development. It was clearly task-oriented.

The lesson required students to find a word from a list of twenty words which best completed the meaning of sentences in a passage. The passage was a summary statement describing the structure and functions of the different parts of Congress. At the beginning of the lesson, Ed reviewed the definitions of the twenty words needed to complete the passage by asking each student in turn to pronounce a

Teacher Observed:	ED		
Date and Time: 3/7 Social Studies Class, 10:30 A.M.			
Observer:			

CORE CONDITION	CRITERIA OR BEHAVIOR OBSERVED		
	Respect		
Teacher Relationships	Ed encourages, he tells Rob about the "pencil eater." Questions are structured and everyone is asked. He cajoles, "Come on, you know this." "You may not know this, we haven't covered it." "Nice guess." Examples are taken from classroom experiences and applied to concept being discussed: amendments and class decision making. Ed demands respect. He encourages others to show it.		
Student Relationships			

Figure 5–11. *Sample from "Global Scale of Teacher Performance."*

word out loud and then tell the class what it meant. Some of the words were House of Representatives, Senate, full term, amendments, and so forth.

The observer was impressed at the high level of respect the teacher and students showed each other. He decided to focus on how this respect was nurtured during the instructional process by looking specifically at how Ed retrieved information from students during this questioning period. A look at a part of the observation instrument, the "Global Scale of Teacher Performance" (see Appendix 2), shows how the observer wrote the observation notes within the instructional task block. A copy of the observer's analysis (see Figure 5–11) is also shown.

It is evident that the observer summarized his notes by listing seven techniques that Ed used to retrieve information from students. The observer carefully portrayed, through the use of examples, how Ed consistently showed respect to students even though he demanded student cooperation and performance on task. An outside reader of this analysis will have little difficulty grasping a picture of how Ed performed. Furthermore, this analysis was developed within two of the three guidelines. First, the observer talks about what he saw, describing Ed's behavior with detailed examples. Second, the feedback is kept to a minimum—only seven items. The third guide is not relevant here because in this consult no suggestions for change were offered. This peer consulting example is completed by revealing a transcript of the conference the teacher and the observer had. A commentary on the dynamics of the discussion is also provided.

Conference

Dialogue

Observer: Hi, Ed, I have here the observation I completed on you yesterday.

Ed: Oh yeah. You know I forgot you were in the room. We were having such a good time.

Observer: Take a minute and read this. (He hands Ed the analysis.

Comments

This is light talk setting the stage and rapport for the conference. The observer reminds Ed of the purpose of the conference and Ed tells the observer that he feels very comfortable with the situation.

The observer here gives Ed a few minutes to read and reflect on what was said. Note only the analysis and not the

Dialogue

Comments

observation instrument was given.

Ed: I did all this?

Ed is impressed with himself and is surprised that he has such a wide repertoire of teaching behavior in this area.

Observer: And more, but I could not put it all down so I concentrated on one single thing. At first I was impressed at how well your students work for you. Then I noticed how you encouraged them. They were answering so many of your questions that I decided I needed to find out what things you did to elicit so much information. You do a lot!

The observer here and in the next statement reinforces Ed and reminds him how impressed he was.

Ed: Well, the class is an excellent group.

Ed tries to give the students the credit. He still denies taking ownership of his excellence.

Observer: Yeah, but I figure if someone came in your room they would first notice how much respect and rapport you have with the students. You probably have heard this before.

Ed: Yeah.

Observer: But here I was interested in finding out how you do it, I mean specifically. I noticed you challenged, used humor, cajoled, and used other procedures I listed to not only gain students' respect but to get them to think.

The observer here tries to make a distinction between previous evaluations Ed may have received and what is described in this analysis. The observer is saying that he tried to get behind the word "respect" and focus on what Ed does.

Ed: I do not know where I learned it. I just do it....

Ed acknowledges here that the observer did indeed do just that. Here he is finally admitting it is his teaching behavior that is good and shows some pride in the fact.

Observer: And well....You see now I can go to Betty and ask her to look at how you use seven different techniques to get students to work. These are excellent instructional behaviors which most would appreciate seeing you employ, in your own way.

The observer already has plans to use Ed's expertise to help Betty. It is obvious that there is a well-established peer consulting team working in the building.

Ed: Well, I see....Thanks for the input. Come again.

Post-Conference

The observer felt she had to convince Ed that the teaching behaviors observed were indeed excellent techniques that Ed performed and not behaviors due to chance or the students. Ed perhaps is too modest about his own ability. Clearly, the observer felt Ed learned a great deal about his teaching style and because of this consciousness could apply these techniques more often and with more effectiveness. The observer felt comfortable with Ed and their exchange reflected the respect they have for each other's talents.

Teacher: Ed
Time: 10 Minutes
Scale: Global Scale of Teacher Performance
Criteria: Use of Various Techniques to Retrieve Information from Students

Ed conducted a large group lesson on government. Each student had a small workbook and was answering questions from a section on the structure of Congress. This lesson was a review of material previously read.

Ed uses a variety of techniques to elicit information from students. These procedures were used continuously, which produced a lively, effective interaction.

1. *Humor:* He asked Rob a question and Rob said he couldn't answer because he had no pencil. Rob said, "The pencil eater has struck." Ed's reply, "Not again!" Rob laughed at this quick uptake and answered the question.

2. *Structure:* Ed asked each student to read and define the vocabulary words needed to complete the close reading section. He made sure the students knew the basics by reviewing them before they attempted to incorporate the information into the task. His structure of the lesson assured high comprehension and cooperative interaction.

3. *Questions:* Ed went around to each student in turn a few times to ask them to read and sound out the vocabulary. His pace was slow and he showed elaborate patience with students. He used his teacher-tutor quite effectively by having her help the student sound out words while he functioned as the task master who put everything on "hold" until the student could respond.

4. *Cajoling:* The use of a lot of coaching terms was evident as Ed forced students to work at the lesson. For example, "Aw, come on, you know how to do this. Try!"

5. *Challenges:* Ed asks the students to go beyond their limits. He forces them to try harder. Example: "You may not know this question because we didn't cover it in class, but try hard to figure it out. You can do it."

6. *Praise:* When a student put down an answer which was later shown to be correct, the student told Ed that he guessed at it. Ed said, "That's right, nice guess. Keep it up!"

7. *Examples:* When students couldn't understand how "amendments" work, Ed used an example which drew from the classroom experience. He carefully showed how committees were needed in the class to get things done, rather than having the whole class get involved in minor decision making. He would ask for further examples.

Figure 5–12. *Classroom observation analysis.*

REFERENCES

Alfonso, Robert J., and Lee L. Goldsberry. "Colleagueship in Supervision," *Association for Supervision and Curriculum Development Yearbook*, Thomas J. Sergiovanni, ed. Alexandria, Virginia: Association for Supervision and Curriculum Development, 1982.

Bolster, Arthur S. "Toward a More Effective Model of Research on Teaching," *Harvard Educational Review, 53*, August 1983, 295–308.

Cogan, Morris L. *Clinical Supervision*. Boston: Houghton-Mifflin, 1973.

Goldhammer, Robert *Clinical Supervision*. New York. Holt, Rinehart and Winston, 1969.

Joyce, Bruce R.; Clark C. Brown; and Lucy Peck, eds. *Flexibility in Teaching*. New York: Longman, 1981.

Maurer, Richard E. "A Proposal to Foster Teaching Skills," The *New York Times*, September 5, 1982, Section II, 18.

Rosenshire, Barak, and Norma Fast. "The Use of Direct Observation to Study Teaching," *Second Handbook of Research on Teaching*, Robert M. W. Travers ed. Chicago: Rand McNally Co., 1973.

Stallings, Jane A. *Learning to Look: A Handbook on Classroom Observation and Teaching Models*. Belmont, California: Wadsworth Co., 1977.

Appendices

APPENDIX 1: TEACHER PERFORMANCE ASSESSMENT INSTRUMENT

There is a consensus that certain teacher behaviors have more of an impact on student performance than others. Most of these behaviors can be defined as the teacher providing direct, highly structured instruction to increase student time-on-task academic behavior. The fifteen teacher behaviors described in this checklist are only a small part of the enormous array of behaviors which teachers perform every day in their classrooms. These are not meant to provide a definitive description of every behavior that works well. Rather, they should be viewed as important teacher behaviors which, when applied effectively, contribute to increased student academic performance.

How to Use the Instrument

It is not essential for you to observe all fifteen of these teacher behaviors at once. In fact, it would be quite a difficult task. It is best to pick one or two of these behaviors to observe in a ten-minute period. Some behaviors such as 1, Frequency Count of Modality Delivery System, and 3, Frequency Count of On-Task Student Behavior, should be observed individually. A detailed description of each behavior, as well as illustrative examples can be found on Chapter 4, "Instructional Strategies."

In this instrument, each teacher behavior is briefly defined operationally, that is, it tells you what the teacher should be doing. In some cases there are many aspects of behavior to be observed. In every case, you will obtain a quantifiable measure of how often you observed the particular behavior. This measure should be reported in the feedback to the teacher. There is also an area under each behavior for a description of what you saw. Your impression of *how* the teacher performs the particular behavior under a particular circumstance is as important to report as the fact that it was done.

TEACHER PERFORMANCE ASSESSMENT INSTRUMENT

1. Frequency Count of Modality Delivery System

The number of times the teacher uses a particular modality to deliver the lesson content.

Visual	The teacher has the students view material or read silently.
Auditory	The teacher speaks to the class or to a student or has the class hear a recording.
Tactile	The teacher has the students write or draw.
Kinesthetic	The teacher has the students act out or role play the content.

Modality (List Each Used)	Time (Record Duration)

2. Frequency Count of Changes in Instructional Format

The number of times the teacher changes the structure of the class to deliver the lesson content. Also, the amount of time spent teaching in a particular format

a. Large group format—The teacher instructs all of the students in the class at the same time. There is no other learning going on at the same time as the teacher's delivery.

b. Small group format—The teacher instructs a small group of students at an assigned place.

c. Seat work format—The students work independently at their desks without direct teacher contact (e.g., workbook assignments).

d. Individualized format—The teacher works one to one with a particular student.

Format (List Each Used)   *Time (Record Duration)*

_____

_____

_____

_____

_____

_____

_____

3. Frequency Count of On-Task Student Behavior

The percentage of students working on task in a particular instructional format. The percentage of student correct responses in a particular instructional format.

a. If the teacher is in a large group format:

> *Instructional level*—At least 90% of the students are maintaining eye contact or are on task with the teacher.
>
> *Frustrational level*—At least 33% of the students are not on task or maintaining eye contact with the teacher.

b. If the teacher is in a small group format.

> *Instructional level*—Student gets at least 80% of the work correct.
>
> *Frustrational level*—Student gets more than 20% of the work correct.

c. If the teacher allows the students to do seat work:

> *Independent level*—The students get at least 80% of their work correct.
>
> *Frustrational level*—The students get more than 20% of the work correct.

d. If the teacher and student are in individualized format:

Frustrational level—The students get 3 errors in 2 minutes.

Instructional Format (List Each Used)	Percent of Students On Task or Percent of Errors
_____	_____
_____	_____ _____
_____	_____
_____	_____

4. Frequency Count of Visual Scanning

The number of times the teacher looks away from the immediate task to look at a student or a group of students.

Record Number: _____

Time Span Measure: _____

Ratio of Scanning (Number::Time): _____

Comments: _____

_____

_____

_____

_____

_____

_____

_____

_____

5. Frequency Count of Active Movement

The number of times the teacher moves about the room to check on the academic work and/or the behavior of the students.

Movement (List Each Activity)	*Reaction* (Comment on Student's Behavior After Movement)

Record Number: _____

Time Span Measured: _____

Ratio of Movement (Number::Time): _____

Comments: _____

_____

_____

_____

_____

6. Frequency Count of Active Questioning

The number of times a teacher asks questions to individual students

Record Number: _____

Time Span Measured: _____

Ratio of Questioning (Number::Time): _____

Comments: _____

_____

_____

_____

_____

_____

_____

7. Frequency Count of Responses to Lesson Interruption

The number of times the teacher either verbally or nonverbally confronts a student or group of students to bring their attention back to the task.

a. *Interruptions* (Check Frequency of Student Behaviors You Consider Interruptions to Lesson.)	*Response* (Did Teacher Respond?)

B. *Response* (List Method Used)	*Time* (Record Duration of Response)	*Effect* (Did Student or Students Stay on Task?)

Comments: _____

_____

_____

_____

_____

_____

_____

_____

_____

_____

_____

8 Frequency Count of Alternating Roles

   a. *Manager roles*—The teacher gives directions, manages the organization of the class, and the flow of the lesson.

   b. *Instructor role*   The teacher delivers information concerning course content.

   c. *Peer role*—The teacher becomes actively involved in the learning situation with students as peers.

Role (List Each Used)	*Time* (Record Duration of Role)	*Effect* (Did Student or Students Stay on Task?)

Comments: _____

_____

_____

_____

_____

_____

_____

_____

_____

_____

_____

_____

_____

_____

9. *Rating of Lesson Clarity*

The rating the observer would give the teacher's lesson presentation in terms of clearness of purpose, effect, and relationship to previous lesson material.

a. Observer's direct rating of clarity of presentation:

1	2	3	4	5
unclear		clear		very clear

b. Observer's rating of the students' understanding of the clarity of lesson's presentation. (Ask two students the following question: "Do you understand what has been taught?" or "Why are you doing this?"

1	2	3	4	5
unclear		clear		very clear

_____

_____

_____

_____

_____

Comments: _____

_____

_____

_____

_____

10. Duration of Transition Time

a. The amount of time the class as a whole takes to change from one lesson (e.g., math) to another (e.g., reading). Measurement from teacher's instruction to initiate a change to time it takes the last student to come to task on the new lesson. _____

Comment on Student Behavior: _____

_____

_____

_____

_____

_____

_____

b. The amount of time a particular student takes upon entering the classroom to the time it takes to come to task on the lesson. _____

Comment on Student Behavior: _____

_____

_____

_____

_____

_____

_____

_____

11. Frequency Count of Review

The number of times the teacher reviews the material taught last month, last week, or yesterday in order to provide the students with an overview of the lesson plans.

_____

_____

_____

Comments. _____

_____

_____

_____

12. Frequency Count of Teacher Followup

The number of homework assignments or independent work assignments the teacher collects or incorporates into the lesson.

_____

_____

_____

_____

_____

_____

_____

13. Presence of Daily Written Schedule of Class Activities

Class Activities

Yes_____   No_____

Did teacher refer to schedule?

Yes_____   No_____

Comments: _____

_____

_____

_____

_____

_____

_____

14. Presence of Posted Class Rules

Yes_____   No_____

Did teacher refer to rules?

Yes_____   No_____

Comments: _____

_____

_____

_____

_____

15. Frequency of Teacher's Praise to the Student

The number of times the teacher offers praise to a particular student for work, for an answer, for thinking ability, or for behavior:

_____

_____

_____

_____

_____

Response (List Each Praise Response)   *Effect* (Comment on Student's Behavior After the Comment)

Comments: _____

_____

_____

_____

_____

_____

_____

_____

_____

_____

_____

_____

_____

APPENDIX 2: GLOBAL SCALE OF TEACHER PERFORMANCE

The observer using this scale has wide latitude in writing an observational report. You are not reporting the frequency of a certain teacher act, but rather the context of how and when the act is used during the lesson. You are looking for clusters of teacher behaviors which, when taken as a whole, produce a certain core condition. These conditions are defined as either task behavior or social relationship behavior. They are:

1. Teacher's Instructional Task
2. Student's Learning Task
3. Teacher's Relationship with Students
4. Student's Relationship to Teacher and Other Students

The questions which need to be asked about the behavioral performance of a teacher will provide an elaborate account of how these core conditions are established and maintained in a classroom. This account, by the nature of the scale, is a subjective judgment by the observer. A subjective opinion is not necessarily a right or wrong opinion. Like all feedback a teacher receives, it should be given careful consideration. The questions to be asked are:

Teacher's Instructional Task: What does the teacher do to promote instruction? What effect does the model of teaching employed have on student rate of learning, responding, or questioning? How does a teacher deliver information to students, and how does the teacher retrieve and have students account for that information?

Student Learning Task: What do the students do to show evidence of learning? How do students give feedback, at what rate, with what success? What effect does increased work time, attendance, appropriate behavior, dress, or language have on student learning? Do students report information by rote, or is it integrated with past information, and if it is, how does this change its perspective?

Teacher's Relationship with Students: What does the teacher do to maintain a relationship with the students? What are the intended and unintended consequences of these behaviors? Does this social behavior contribute to student learning? If so, what effect does increased student learning have on the teacher's perspective of the students? How does the teacher differentiate among students in social contacts? Is it evident, necessary, and accepted? How does the teacher confront off-task behavior?

Student Relationship to Teacher and to Other Students: How does a student or group of students use social contacts with other students to communicate to a teacher, about what? Do social cliques contribute to or hinder student learning and how does a teacher deal with them? How do students attempt to take the leadership from the teacher and what is the teacher's response to this process?

How to Use This Scale

First decide which of the four core conditions you would like to observe. Second, pick a specific criterion around which you will cluster the teacher's behavior. A partial list of criteria is provided below. For example, to determine how students show evidence of learning, you might choose the criterion of "energy" to focus on. Third, write the chosen criterion in the small box provided on the top of the scale. A second box is provided if you wish to observe two criteria at once. The fourth step is to observe the performance of the teacher and record under the chosen criterion next to the chosen condition everything you feel the teacher does which contributes to the criteria of fostering this core condition. In our example, you will need to record those selected teacher/student behaviors which provide the dynamism to lesson learning. A ten- to fifteen-minute observation period will provide you with a wealth of information.

Selected criteria or teacher behavior to observe are

Energy	Touch	Cooperation
Timing	Eye Contact	Trust
Power	Movement	Praise
Pace	Questioning	Review
Goal Orientation	Task Standards	Values
Delivery System	Voice Tone	Room Environment
Planning	Warmth	Board Work

Teacher Observed: _____

Date and Time: _____

Observer: _____

CRITERIA OR BEHAVIOR OBSERVED		
CORE CONDITION		
Instructional Task		
Learning Task		

Global Scale of Teacher Performance

Teacher Observed: _____
Date and Time: _____
Observer: _____

CORE CONDITION	CRITERIA OR BEHAVIOR OBSERVED
Teacher Relationships	
Student Relationships	

Global Scale of Teacher Performance

Index